I0202137

THIS GODLY

CHILD OF MINE

Copyright © 2014 by Marricke Kofi Gane

THIS GODLY CHILD OF MINE

By Marricke Kofi Gane

ISBN: 978-1-909326-24-8

All rights reserved solely by the author. The author guarantees all contents are original and do not infringe upon the legal rights of any other person or work. No part of this book may be reproduced in any form without the permission of the author. For permission requests and others, write to the Author at:

author@marrickekofigane.com

Published by MarrickeGanePublishing

Distributed by Amazon

THIS GODLY
CHILD OF MINE

*How To Raise A Godly Child
In An Increasingly Perverse
And Lawless World*

By Marricke Kofi GANE

Contents

INTRODUCTION ix

1   TRAINING A CHILD TO GO… GO WHERE? 1

2   LET'S TRAIN YOU UP, MY CHILD (THE METHOD) 7

3   TRAIN UP A CHILD, NOT AN ADULT 33

4   THIS IS THE WAY TO GO (THE CONTENT) 43

5   IT'S ALL ABOUT THE CHILD 93

6   20 PATRIARCH PRAYERS FOR CHILDREN 109

AUTHOR'S OTHER WORKS 119

ABOUT THE AUTHOR 123

DEDICATION

To my wife and all mothers out there:

Your commitment, is instruction to our children,

your patience, is strength to their destinies,

your love, is oil that graces their heads,

your prayer is order to their path.

May they and the generations

beyond rise and call you

BLESSED.

INTRODUCTION

Raising a child is by all means a very grave responsibility – it is indeed grave beyond the need to simply provide them with food and shelter. It is grave because: In them is the answer of God, to the prayers of the world; in them is the future of many generations yet unborn; in them is the hope of nations and countless peoples – and as parents, we stand between their manifestation and demise.

In Psalm 127: 3–4 the Bible declares

"Behold, children are a heritage from the Lord, the fruit of the womb is a reward. <u>Like arrows in the hand of a warrior</u>, so are the children of one's youth."

Well, neither an inheritance nor a reward is of any use if it cannot add value to the life of the man or woman in whose hands it falls or if s/he cannot add value to it either. In the same manner, where a warrior is concerned, an arrow is of no benefit to his greatness if he does not know how it is shot. And therein lies the revelation – arrows are made to be shot; whether to send or receive a message, whether to attack with, whether as a weapon of defence – they are made to be shot. And until it is shot, it neither qualifies as an arrow nor a thing of value in the hand of a warrior.

Children are born into the bosom of parents to be *"trained up"* as the Bible teaches in Proverbs 22:6 *"Train up a child in the way he should go and when he is old he will not depart from it."* There is a precise way an arrow has to be shot in order that it has the most impact, but even better, *there is a way* a child should be trained up to go, so that s/he, when grown, may have the most impact in the earth and bring the most glory to God.

As long as children are not trained up in *"the way they should go,"* our world will continue to see waywardness and grave disappointments, especially in the lives of those children we most expected to turn out for the good – it is not the fault of the children, it is the way they were trained up to go.

In this book, the Spirit of God has taken me on my most humbling journey yet. A journey that has brought with it true insights into how to train up His children to grow up into impactful, significant and glorious citizens of His Kingdom. It is a very practical book and yet, rooted in the very word of God Almighty. It is my solemn prayer that as you read this book and apply its principles, the children God has blessed us all with, will grow upwards towards God; upwards away from the filth below and upwards away from the waywardness beneath. May the hand of the LORD God Almighty be upon us all and may He lead us to teach our children to number their days and apply their hearts to wisdom. Amen.

Purely as a matter of convenience in writing, wherever I have referred to a person as masculine, I most equally also imply the feminine and vice versa.

Marricke K. Gane
Author

I

TRAINING A CHILD TO GO... **GO WHERE?**

Many Christian and even non-Christian parents or guardians have most likely come across this very popular text in the Bible - Proverbs 22:6. It says *"Train up a child in the way he should go and when he is old he will not depart from it."* Personally, and am sure many others, also find this piece of scripture very profound. It sums up very concisely four very delicate truths about how each man or woman will turn out in life based on certain unchanging parameters:

Firstly, the real work involved in setting up a child to become a significant and successful man or woman is in *"training them up."* Notice it isn't just *"train"* but rather *"train up,"* signifying that there is also an alternative approach by which one can be *"trained down."* The problem that most of us face as parents, is in trying to find a match between what we want our children to learn and the type of training needed to deliver such learning. It is essential we recognise as Christian parents, that the difference between the way we train our children and the way the world train theirs is that the outcome of our training must lead our children *"upwards" (train up)*. Up, towards God; up, away from the filth below; up, to soar like the eagles in life's endeavours; up, so that they become examples for the rest of the world to look up to.

Secondly, that there is such a thing as *"the way"* – we cannot afford to train them any other way, but *"the way."* In other words, there is a particular way in which a child must be trained to go and only when he is trained in that way will he NOT depart from it. The *"way"* being referred to does not only relate to the method, but also the content of the training.

Thirdly, it is essential that the training is done when he is a child, not when he's fully grown. This in itself is a very apparent truth both practically, spiritually and psychologically. Children naturally have a higher learning and absorption capacity than adults, but quite apart from that, it is also evident that habits, patterns and lifestyles formed very early in life are harder to break than those formed in later life.

Lastly, the child should be trained in the way *"he"* should go – not the way the father wants to go, not the way the mother wants to go, not the way the teachers and community want him to go – "...in the way *HE* should go..." Of a necessity, everything involved in training up a child should accommodate his peculiar strengths, his individual ability and generally everything that makes him the unique child or person that he is.

The text *"...and when he is old, he will not depart from it"* is really just the outcome of the above four inputs. The implication is that you can predictably tell the core outcomes of a person's adult life by understanding these four areas of inputs during their childhood.

God planted a garden, but it was Adam's duty to till it. Exactly in the same way God blesses us with children, but it is our duty to "till," to "keep" and to "prune" them. If Adam had decided to do nothing but let nature take its course, the beautiful garden would have become an overgrown den, because believe it or not – nature's only natural course of action is towards entropy (i.e. deterioration).

There are many cases in our world today of young people and adults alike with awfully bad characters, moral failures, unfulfilled destinies and on and on. For this group of people, society, families, communities and even nations spend fortunes trying to correct their lives – needless to say, we've got it wrong. The truth is, we should not have waited for them to grow out of childhood and veer from "*the way they should go*" before we waste time, emotions and money trying to redirect them. Most of the failed lives the world produces are testaments to failed parenthood. That's a hard fact – but it's true. God gave the blueprint for raising successful men and women. Everything you do outside that plan has an unpleasant consequence.

I will not attempt to be naïve and say everyone who turns out in life differently to what God purposed for them did so because of wrong training, but likely eight out of ten times, I am confident it resulted from one or more of these four:

(i)   That they were not *"trained up"* but rather just *"trained"* or *"trained down"*

(ii) That they were not trained when they were a *"child"* – it was done a little too late.

(iii) That they may have been trained, but not *"in the way"* that he should go

(iv) That they may have been trained, but not in the way *"HE"* should go. They may have been trained in the way their parents or guardians wanted to go; not considering the child's uniqueness.

In the following chapters, we will attempt to look in more detail at the various components of raising a child including the methods, the frameworks and the content – the God way.

2

LET'S **TRAIN YOU UP**, MY CHILD (THE METHOD)

Any parent or guardian who has ever had any form of formal school education will agree that you could have two or more schools all running the same syllabus, same physical conditions and yet, a few of those schools *(so-called elites)* will consistently produce students with good results whilst the others struggle – it's all in the delivery. Or you can equally imagine a child performing badly in a certain school and suddenly, he is transferred to another school – and he begins to do remarkably well – it really is all in the delivery.

If you are reading this book, then I don't need to tell you that the Bible is a phenomenal book. More excitingly, it teaches us as parents, guardians and leaders, five very clear methods through which children need to be trained-up. Before I proceed to show the five different methods shown in the Bible, it is important to clarify this – the Hebrew language, in which the Old Testament was originally written, is a hugely complicated yet very rewarding language. Understanding it opens a world of scriptural revelations that cannot be emphasised enough. It is not a coincidence that it is the language in which God chose to communicate His eternal truths to us. Christians who choose to willingly ignore the treasures of understanding the Old Testament in its original language and merely justify it by saying *"nobody needs Hebrew for revelation"* are only cheating themselves out of understanding some of the treasures of God's word. In the same manner, one would have asked *"why then do we also need any language to communicate with God?"*

The methods of training-up a child that will be laid out here are derived from certain specific Hebrew words in the Old Testament

used to refer to the phrase "train-up." Unfortunately, due to the limitations of the English language, most of the meanings of the phrase
"train up," were somewhat lost in translation and merely translated
into regular words such as *"teach, instruct, chastise, lead, show etc."*
Inasmuch as these words will still be used as we go along, I will try
and reveal the true meanings of the methods of *training-up* a child
by creating mental pictures that you can identify with. Here we go:

Yarah

1 Samuel 20:20 – *"Then I will **shoot (Yarah)** three arrows to
the side, as though I shot at a target"* (remember the Bible talks
about children being like arrows in the hands of a warrior in
Psalm 127:4?)

The word *"yarah"* is one of the Hebrew words used to depict the
phrase *"train up."* It means, *"to throw"* or *"to shoot..* I want you to
imagine the scenario as described in the passage of 1 Samuel 20.
Jonathan is telling David he will *shoot* an arrow and the idea being
conveyed here, is that David ought to *"LOOK"* in the direction the
arrow is headed.

Consider you have located an item in the distance and you were
trying to show someone where the item was located. It may be very
difficult for them to see what you are trying to get them to see if
you had just nodded or gestured with your head in the direction
of the item. On the contrary, if you picked up a piece of stone and

threw it in the exact direction of the item or if you shot an arrow next to the item, you would have enabled your companion to follow the trajectory of the stone *(or arrow)* to where the item is located, hence narrowing the scope of places s/he would have wrongly been looking at.

Now, the Bible is not teaching us to use arrows as a method of showing your children what direction they ought to be headed in life. It is only a pictorial illustration of how to show them a certain direction in which they ought to head. The illustration above can equally be related to you figuratively *"throwing"* your finger or pointing your finger in a specific, chosen, direction as in Exodus 15:24-25 – *"And the people complained against Moses, saying, "What shall we drink? "So he cried out to the Lord, and the Lord **showed** (yarah) him a tree. When he cast it into the waters, the waters were made sweet."*

Essentially, this method of training-up a child also involves *"pointing them to where they should be headed."*

It is necessary when pointing out the way to a child that two things are always borne in mind. In fact in the absence of these two criteria, you haven't really succeeded in pointing the child to anything. Firstly, remember that when you shoot an arrow, throw a stone or point a finger *(figuratively)* to your child – it has to be at a target. The target has either got to land exactly where the child needs to go to or the closest possible to it. Secondly, wherever the target you are showing your child is and whatever the trajectory of the method deployed, neither must take them outside the word of God, His will or presence.

The question is begged – *"in a practical sense, how do I 'point my child in a direction?"* By noting the amazing lessons we can learn from visualising the process of showing a child something at a distance, by shooting an arrow or pointing a finger:

(i)   You have to first know the exact location of the target *(possibly from past experiences and or encounters)*. This has a responsibility for us as parents or guardians and it is this – you cannot use this method to train-up a child if the target you are trying to get them to is not one you are personally familiar with.

(ii)   You don't need to go to the target yourself – you can lead the child to a target by shooting an arrow, throwing a stone or pointing a finger from a distance. In other words, there are tools *(the arrow, the stone, the finger)* you can use to move your child from their current ignorance about the target location, to the position of *(and eventually their)* knowledge of the target location. These tools may include things like specific formal education, books, videos, written instructions, instructions through conversations, instructions through demonstration etc.

(iii) Note a very important part of *"pointing"* your child to a certain end – it really shouldn't end at just pointing it out to them. You have to watch them walk or run towards it.

Then comes the last and most important part of this method
– direct them as they go along until they get to the target.
Remember that you are still in the unique position of not
only knowing where the target is, but you can also see from
a distance whether the child is walking towards the target
or veering too far away from it. This is where most parents,
guardians and leaders miss it – they throw the stone to show
their children the target and then leave them on their own to
waddle all the way to the target. This is not to say you need to
be screaming instructions at them every step of the way. No,
that wouldn't help them grow. But it is helpful that you are
on hand to give them a slight nudge if they are veering too
far away from the target, and sometimes, if necessary, you
may just have to throw another stone, shoot another arrow
or point another finger.

It is worth considering the following – that after you have pointed the
child to the target, the next biggest step is that you *"allow"* them to
head off towards such a target. At this point they are likely to be on
their own *(even though you will be watching from a distance)*. It makes
this method, one to primarily apply in the areas that you need a child
to develop self-mastery, self-confidence, or ability to work out their
own way of moving from the receipt of direction to the application
of it.

Alaph

Proverbs 22:24-25 – *"Make no friendship with an angry man, and with a furious man do not go, lest you **learn (Alaph)** his ways and set a snare for your soul"*

The word *"Alaph"* is another Hebrew word used to clarify the term *"train up."* It means *"to yoke together"* and it is derived from the Hebrew word for an ox – *"Eleph."* In a sense therefore, the word *"Alaph"* means yoking two oxen together. So what has this got to do with training up a child? Well, in modern agriculture, ploughing, which forms the fundamental of land cultivation, is done using a tractor. In Biblical era however, ploughing a farm was done by yoking two oxen together on the neck and attaching a plough behind them. What many people don't realise is that an older, mature and more experienced ox was always yoked with younger inexperienced ox. The latter will over time, learn from the older by association. And there, you have the second way of training a child – by association with a more experienced adult or person(s).

Needless to say there are several examples of this method of training in the Bible. Just to mention a few: Elisha was yoked with Elijah and in the end caught a double portion of Elijah's Spirit; Samuel was yoked with Eli to become a prophet; Joshua was yoked with Moses and later successfully led Israel into the promise land.

Interestingly, this method of yoking and learning by association used to be very prevalent in the times of old especially where grooming of young adults was concerned. Today, even though it is not a common phenomenon anymore, there are still grooming schools in Switzerland, Britain and some parts of the United States, where young people are sent to become refined gentlemen and ladies. And the process is simply as described for ploughing in Biblical times – inexperienced children are yoked to mature and more accomplished aristocrats. But beyond that, learning by association is a very practical method that any parent can use to train up their children in the things that need to be mastered very early in life.

At the time of writing this book, my wife and I will always lay our hands on our little daughter every morning and bless her before I leave for work. Suddenly one day, after I blessed her, she also stretched her hands towards my head and said *"in the na na Jesus, Amen."* I said Amen; we clapped for her and praised her *"Good girl! Good girl!"* Subsequently, every day after I bless her, I ask her to bless me too. She is just eighteen months old and it wouldn't be coincidence that she will grow up forming a habit of praying for her children some day. Nothing is a coincidence. She was yoked to her parents and she learnt what we did, within that association.

A few things are worth noting here. Firstly, children by association will learn from their parents as they are the very first older oxen they are yoked to from birth *(so to speak).* Whether the parents consider that they have all that is needed for their children to learn by association, in order for them to be fully equipped for their future is a decision that must not be taken lightly. What is worth saying however, is that God being so wise and knowing that He was creating more than one human being, did not place ALL things in one man – so that we can relate and depend on one another for completeness. In my personal experience as a child, there were *occasions (as part of our family's holiday system)* that I was shipped off several times to my father's best friend's family to spend long vacations and their children vice versa. I remember so clearly my father would always tell his friend not to treat me differently to his children during my stay. I can confidently say today *(quite happily too)* that there are things I have learnt from that family that have shaped my life in a good way and added to me as a better person.

For parents, it takes a lot more than just love, to come to the realisation that you don't single handedly have *"everything"* your child needs to be fully equipped for life's journey and to look for someone who has that missing ingredient to impact your children. A few things need to be considered:

(i)   You need to know what exactly it is you don't have, but which your children need to learn in order to make them complete for their life's journey. Please understand we are not only referring to spiritual things, but also to things as basic as life skills, traits and abilities.

(ii)   Recognising whether you *(both)* as parents have it in you, in its best form, to impart it to your children by association. This is not something to feel bad about. The truth is that we all don't have it all but on a positive note, there are some excellent, learnable things that you may also have that others don't have. Making this honest assessment is proof to both yourselves and your children that you are committed to looking beyond your imperfections to make your children closer to perfect. And God will indeed reward you for being a good steward.

(iii) You need to carefully find who has what it is you want your children to be impacted with and establish their willingness to be yoked with your children for such an impartation. My only advice here is that you, as much as possible, have to be unbiased. This really isn't about you but your children. It isn't about your liking or not liking somebody, even if they possess what your children need and if they are willing to impart it. It is about putting aside your personal issues so that your children are NOT denied access to a successful future.

Shanan

Deuteronomy 6:6-7 – *"And these words which I command you today shall be in your heart. You shall **teach them diligently (Shanan)** to your children, and shall talk of them when you sit in your house, when you walk by the way, when you lie down, and when you rise up"*

The third Hebrew word used to explain the method of teaching is *"Shanan"* which literally translates as *"to sharpen"* – just like a knife or sword is sharpened. Of course in today's *(fast)* world, it merely takes a grinding machine to be turned on for less than five or so minutes and your otherwise blunt knife would have been sharpened. In the days of old, this wasn't the case. Sharpening a knife took the long, patient and diligent process of rubbing the blunt knife in long careful strides against a stone or another metal. Hence in Proverbs 27:17, the writer declares *"As iron sharpens (shaman) iron, so a man sharpens (shaman) the countenance of his friend."*

A blunt knife cuts nothing, and if it does, you need to apply a greater amount of strength than is normally required for it to happen. In the same manner if certain skills and attributes of your child are NOT sharpened, it will take a lot more unnecessary effort when they grow up to make an impact both in their own life and in the life of others. As is described in the Deuteronomy passage above, sharpening your child is a long diligent process – and this gives direct insight into which aspects of our children's lives we can apply this type of training method to. These are the aspects of their lives that should not be expected to simply change over a few days. They are areas of their lives that are engrained in their natural fabric and which will thus require a slow, patient and diligent approach to shaping up.

I was blessed enough in my youth to have the experience of sharpening knives using a piece of rock that my grandpa had in his compound strictly for that purpose *(the blessing came from the fact that my grandparents weren't high-tech back then)*. It is worth noting a few crucial things that we should learn from the manual sharpening process and how it can be translated into a training method that will be a blessing to our children and future generations:

(i)   The first thing to bear in mind is the objective for wanting to sharpen a knife. In this context, your child – if they are blunt, they cannot cut through life or even if they did, they would do so by expending a great deal of effort, at the end of which they would have been too weary to even appreciate, let alone enjoy their God given accomplishments.

(ii) It is worth understanding that whatever is to be sharpened already exists. The knife to be sharpened already exists. The process of sharpening does not suddenly produce the knife, but instead it works on an already existent knife. In other words, this method of training is not one to be deployed where a new learning needs to be imparted to your child. No, this process involves taking what your child already has and sharpening it. It is therefore essential that you identify, if the nature, traits, abilities etc. that you wish to sharpen in your child, are already in their possession. If they aren't, then this is not a method to apply.

(iii) One of the crucial elements of the sharpening process is that as you continually press and rub the knife against the piece of rock *(or metal) or grinder*, tiny bits of the knife wear off from the edge being sharpened. This defines exactly what should happen to your child in order for them to be sharpened – the parts of their nature, personalities, traits etc. that currently makes them blunt need to be CAREFULLY grinded off. I used the word "carefully" here because, you need to remember you simply don't want to grind the whole knife away – just the fragments that are making it blunt.

(iv)   This manual *(or should I say primitive but useful)* sharpening process, interestingly has something in common with the modern method of using an electric sharpening machine and it is this – you have to press the knife against the grinding stone by applying measured pressure. If the pressure is low, the knife won't sharpen and if it is more than required, the knife will simply wear off instead of sharpening. In the case of our children, it translates first to understanding that the process of sharpening them must involve some pressure. Certainly from my experience, some good prolonged pressure from my parents successfully grinded off me, things like laziness, unhealthy competition, selfishness etc. We are referring to a good measure of consistent parental pressure in the form of repetitions, reiterations, insistencies, firmness and to a measured extent, some inflexibility, until those rough edges grind away. Do remember all the time, that the pressure must not be too much as to let your child feel *"crushed,"* in which case, instead of having the desired effect, it could have a horrible counter effect of spurring them into rebellion. Neither should it be too weak and thus have the effect of your children seeing you as "not serious."

(v)   Certainly, the grinder against which the knife is being rubbed *(sharpened)* has to be stronger than the knife itself. That is a necessity – otherwise, the undesirable edges of the knife won't wear off and there would be no sharpening. So what exactly is the stone, the rock, the grinder or the other metal that you are trying to sharpen your child against? You may have guessed that already, but if you haven't, it is the stronger standard their sharpness will be measured by. Realistically, you must know when a knife is sharp, because if you don't know where to stop, you'll just grind that knife to breaking point. This standard can be communicated to your child *(if s/he can understand you enough)* through examples, comparisons, associations, contrasts, illustrations etc. It is vital the child should be made to know what the destination is or to put it jokingly, why you are rubbing him/her under pressure the way you are. This is so s/he can also feel some sense of accomplishment on reaching that destination. Do lavish them with encouragement when they make it.

(vi) Finally, when you are sharpening a knife on a piece of rock or on another metal, you always do so with intermittent sprinkles of water. The word of God must be part of this entire process. In fact without it, you shouldn't even start the process. It simply means that (i) you must pray through the word of God for this training of your child to be successful and most importantly, proactively pray over the child for the hand of God to help in the moulding process (ii) the motive for wanting to sharpen your child in the areas chosen MUST align with God's word and (iii) the standards you apply in sharpening your child, whether they are role model men or women or events, all have to agree with the standards of the Bible.

Every child, irrespective of the perfection with which they were born, will at some point in their growing childhood, need to be trained by *"sharpening" (shanan)*. The passage in Proverbs 27:17 leads us to appreciate that one of the core areas of our children's nature that needs sharpening is their *"countenance."* This does not refer to countenance as in the *physical appearance* of a person, but rather their inner ability to control temperament and exercise composure. It is these two abilities, depending on which one is stronger, that eventually reflects in the outer countenance we see as joy, peace, anger etc.

Yasar

Proverbs 29:17 – *"**Correct (Yasar)** your son and he will give you rest; yes, he will give delight to your soul"*

Proverbs 3:12 – *"For whom the LORD loves He* **Corrects (Yasar)***, just as a father the son in whom he delights"*

"Yasar" means two things, and both of them are very closely related. Firstly it means *"to turn someone from one direction to another"* and it also means *"to turn someone's head."* It subtly means *"to correct"* but I prefer that we stick with the way God intended us to understand it – to turn the head of someone or turn them onto another direction. This method of training up a child requires equal doses of being pro-active and being firm, but not one or the other – both.

The concept of training up by *"Yasar"* inherently assumes that the child is already in motion, but heading in the wrong direction. The need for proactivity on the part of the parent stems out of love *(Proverbs 3:12)*. You don't have to wait for your child to continue in the wrong path until s/he falls into a ditch of life before administering recovery – the sad, yet blatant truth is that anyone who falls, *(whether a child, a seasoned Christian, a Minister of God)*, never rises to the same level as they were before the fall – you'll always lose something from falling. And there isn't any guarantee that what you lost would be acquired back in its original state of uniqueness.

I can understand someone reading this may be wondering and saying to themselves, *"Oh well, but children are too young to fall into life's ditches etc."* Well, if for example, your child has very subtly started beating his siblings at every little opportunity and if you don't pro-actively start dealing with it before it transforms into a regular habit, you are pretty much allowing him to *"fall"* into the habit of using his hands wrongly. Don't be surprised if he starts fighting you or beating his wife in the future – even though he is still a Christian. He fell as a child. Indeed there has been a misconception in the body of Christ that *"to fall"* only relates to sinning. No, it doesn't – it relates to being in any position lower than what God would have you be in. A man's hands are to be lifted up in prayer, provide comfort, protection and sustenance for his dependents. That is the position of a man's hands ordained by God; any use other than these denotes a *"fall"*.

Earlier, we indicated the need to not only be proactive but also firm. Please understand that, everyone is sustained on the path they are on by their will, irrespective of whether such a path is right or wrong. Wherever you decide to walk to, it is your will that sustains your commitment to such a path. When a parent recognises a wrong path being plied by their child and engages in the process of either *"turning their heads" (Yasar)* in the right direction or *"turning them from their wrong path onto a new path" (also Yasar),* they are doing so by going in the opposite direction to the child's will. This conflict of wills creates resistance and the parents' ability to be firm in their own will, determines whether or not that child eventually falls or is rescued and redirected.

There are a few things that parents need to understand in applying the Yasar approach to training up a child in the way they should go:

(i)   Some ways of teaching require that the parent *(teacher)* be in front, so that the child *(student)* can learn from observation and imitation. The correction *(Yasar)* approach demands that you lead from behind the child. It is more supervisory than front row leadership. It requires that the child be allowed to be proactive and take the initiative. It requires minimal interference unless at the point where you are certain that there is a ditch ahead and that the general direction of the child is very likely to end him/her up in such a ditch.

(ii) The correction *(Yasar)* method requires parents' understanding of the path being plied by their child and more importantly a good idea of where it is leading. It is the only way you can know whether a fall is imminent by them continuing in that path, or not. It is worth sounding a warning here, that although a parent has an understanding of the path their child is plying, they shouldn't oblige the child to walk in the exact path and in the exact way the parent would have walked it. That is why you are teaching from behind rather than from the front. So long as the child is generally in the right direction, it is fine – allow them to develop their independence and confidence and the ability to make guided decisions, which by the way is not the same as imposed decisions.

When we explained the meaning of the word Yasar earlier, we understood it meant to turn one's head or to turn their direction. What this means is that part of the process should involve a mental redirection *(i.e. the head)* and partly an attitudinal redirection *(i.e. turning the whole body)*. In other words, when you do conclude that your child needs a change from a certain way of doing things; you need to redirect both their thinking and attitude. And remember, you need to do this proactively and firmly.

So how exactly, do you correct *(Yasar)* a child in order to turn his head away from the wrong direction to the correct one? – By rebuke, discipline, deprivation or restraint.

I suppose the easiest way of seeing the picture is to perhaps ask you to assume that your child was walking towards the edge of a very high cliff and that when s/he gets to the edge s/he was likely to continue walking right over it. Assume also that you are walking ten feet behind them. What would you do to stop them from falling over the edge? If you can't first stop them walking off the cliff, you can't redirect them. In fact redirection is the easy part. I certainly am no mind reader but I won't be far from wrong if some of the ideas that have cropped up in your wild imagination would include:

(i)   You may use your voice to call loudly at him/her, asking them to stop walking or turn around *(that's rebuke)*

(ii)   Throw a rope around them, pulling them back before they reach the cliff or perhaps even desperately throw yourself forward and grab them by the leg to prevent them walking over *(that's restraint)*

(iii) Or you might walk and overtake them, stand in front of them and prevent them from walking   any further *(that's deprivation)*

(iv) Or you may actually push them heavily to fall flat on the ground before they even reach the cliff *(that's punishment)*

I will resist the temptation of having to delve into types of punishment. I trust that each parent will find a commensurate and appropriate way of applying Yasar to their children.

Lamad

Deuteronomy 4:10 – *"Remember the day you stood before the Lord your God in Horeb, when the Lord said to me, 'gather the people to Me and I will let them hear My words, that they may learn to fear Me all the days they live on the earth and that they may **teach (Lamad)** their children."*

Finally, the fifth Hebrew method of learning is Lamad. The word *"Lamad"* means *"to direct."* It comes from the word *"Lemad"* which means the staff of a shepherd. Effectively therefore, *"Lamad"* can be interpreted to mean, learning by directing with a staff.

Without any hesitation, I'd like to say that any objective of training up a child in the way they should go, which does not include this method of training and learning has failed. And I offer no apologies for that.

This perhaps is the most important and most straightforward method of training, but the least considered in many Christian homes. It is about time we start understanding as parents that the fact that we are Christian parents does not automatically mean our children will grow towards God. We need to consciously grow them towards God. It is indeed a conscious work and using the Lamad approach is a key in that work. A few critical things to bear in mind about this method are that:

(i)   The rod/staff of the shepherd is primarily responsible for directing the sheep. It is essential, to understand before we proceed further, that the rod or staff of a shepherd is not only used to direct his sheep, but also to defend them against predators, pull them out of ditches and much more. The staff in the case of the Christian parent is the word of God. In 2 Timothy 3:16 the Bible declares *"All Scripture is given by inspiration of God, and is profitable for doctrine, for reproof, for correction, for **instruction** in righteousness."* So just as the staff of a shepherd has many purposes, the primary one of which is to direct, likewise, the word of God has many purposes, the primary one of which is to instruct *(direct)* our children upwards towards God. The most practical way of doing this is to ensure that (a) as many questions as a child asks receives answers that are drawn from stories or instances in the Bible that you have previously told them and (b) every correction, direction and redirections you administer to them is backed by a story or instance from the Bible. This conscious approach to connecting the Bible to their everyday lives and the reasoning behind all or most actions draws them into unconsciously accepting the word of God as part of their daily life, and thus a core element of their regular living. The word of God must never be a "new addition" to life along the way. It must be the life all the way.

(ii) Secondly, recognise the staff is always in the hand of the shepherd. The staff by itself cannot direct, defend, retrieve etc. – it has to be in the hand of the shepherd. This means, we as parents, of a necessity need to have a good grasp of the word of God. If we don't, there is simply no way we can apply it in every practical situation as indicated in (i) above. Simply no way. In Exodus 4:20 the Bible refers, to the staff in Moses' hand as the *"rod of God."* Interestingly however, it used to merely be *"a rod"* in Moses' hand, until Moses came to the understanding that the rod in his hand was the authority of God by which he was to direct all of Israel out of Egypt into the promised land – then all of a sudden, the Bible stopped referring to it as a rod but rather as *"the rod of God."* You must resolve that you will have a hold on the word of

God and by it alone will your children be directed. Practically resolve that you will tell them stories from the Bible and that you will go back to those stories many times over to answer their questions, give them directions, redirect them and inspire them. But whatever you do, let it come from the Word of God.

(iii)   Finally, when a shepherd directs his sheep with a staff, he does so by prodding the sheep with his rod: remind your child from day to day about what you have previously taught them from the Bible. I personally suggest that every time you read them stories or teach them new things from the Bible, connect such teachings with life lessons. When that is all done, prod them daily with the word – ask them questions to bring to memory daily, what you taught them previously from the Word of God. Never let their minds forget the lessons from the Word. Play games with the word and make it fun. *"Who can tell me three things that we learnt from the story of Samson"* – each correct answer wins a chocolate or something. Prod them with the word but don't break their ribs.

In summary, the five main Godly methods for training up a child in the way to go are:

(i)   *Yarah* – by pointing at the destination the child should head to.

(ii)   *Alaph* – by yoking together to learning by association.

(iii) *Shanan* – by sharpening or grinding away unwanted parts.

(iv)   *Yasar* – by correction or redirection or turning away.

(v)   *Lamad* – by directing with the word of God.

3

TRAIN UP **A CHILD**, NOT AN ADULT

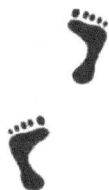

The Bible is a very specific book, meaning that it says things exactly as God wants it said – nothing more, nothing less. It is for this reason in Deuteronomy 4:2 and in many other places in the scriptures, we are commanded not to add or take away from it, because doing so will lose the meaning God intended for us. So, when we read Proverbs 22:6 ***"Train up a child in the way he should go and when he is old, he will not depart from it,"*** we ought to understand that it is not a coincidence that God requires us to train up a person when he is a child. It is that simple – training is best received as a child. I will now proceed to give some reasons why it is essential to train up a person when they are a child.

Children Equal Total Retention:

I could pretty much write this paragraph alone and conclude it as the sole reason why we are instructed to deliver training to a child and not an adult. Even I, was fascinated when I found out. For a while I had been researching why the Bible had been very specific about training children as a pre-requisite for a successful life and then, one day in my study of the Torah it dawned on me. Of course, it was sitting in front of me all the while – the Hebrew word for a child is *"na`ar"*.

The word *"na`ar"* apart from meaning a *"child"* as we know it in English, also means something more revealing – it also means *"Retainer."* This is absolutely in line with scientific discoveries. Child psychologists have found that a child's brain acts like a hungry sponge, soaking up everything that is fed to it. But here it was; the Bible had it thousands of years before psychology researchers started working on children. How amazing. Yes, the word is *"retainer."* That's how God himself wanted children described. No wonder he instructed them to be trained at this tender age, because it is at this age that their ability to retain is at its peak.

This understanding puts enormous responsibility on parents to appreciate that you can't afford to take children for granted. They are magnets that don't lose their polarity. They will retain everything they see, hear, smell, touch or taste. There are times that my wife and I have talked in the presence of our little daughter Otzara, whilst she is seated in the corner of the living room playing by herself and to our amazement, a week or sometimes, weeks later, she repeats to us randomly, some of the very words we used in that one or three week old conversation – and there we were, thinking she was busy playing, yet, because of the retaining nature of her child-like state, nothing goes away unabsorbed.

This realisation of the true, God-inspired nature of children is equally a call on Godly parents not to underestimate which parts of the Godly curriculum to train children in. Don't say they are not at that age yet. Teach them all things God – it will be retained. It may not be exhibited back to you immediately, but you can be certain that it was retained.

In a Child, the Training Ingredient is Virgin:

Let us understand that training is not the same as education. In fact a person can be educated and remain untrained. Education is a process that makes a certain type or types of knowledge available to an individual. It is more or less like filling up an empty individual with some foreign matter. Foreign in the sense that he or she was never created with it. Education is the same for everybody who receives that type of knowledge.

So, you may hear phrases such as *"she was educated in the sciences"* meaning she has been given a knowledge of a particular science. That is why say in a science, or business or arts school, the science, business or arts syllabi is the same for all students who go through such a school. Every one of them will be fed the same curriculum. It is a knowledge base that will be common to all of them. Education does not go as far as figuring out how each student processes the knowledge within their individual selves – it merely ends at ensuring that everybody is exposed to or filled with the same knowledge. That's education.

On the contrary, training, firstly doesn't fill a person or expose children to any foreign matter. Instead, training involves using their internal strengths and inherent abilities to mould them into persons of significance. In truth, training cannot happen without first identifying a person's strength or inherent abilities, because that is really what training is about – to sharpen their inherent abilities and to consolidate their latent strengths. And therein lies why training is best done when a person is a child – because as a child, it is easiest to spot a person's strengths and inherent abilities.

As a child, a person's raw God-given abilities are in their purest, virgin states and can be clearly identified. At this stage of their lives, they have not had much exposure to *"our world"* and hence their abilities have not yet been trampled on by disapprovals, diluted by the need to conform, corrupted by worldly philosophies or wasted through non-optimisation. It is crucially important to understand, that just like in making the best of any food, ingredients are best used in their freshest forms, so also training is best served when its most important ingredient of raw abilities is freshest in childhood.

Training Requires Faith:

In Luke 18:17 we read *"Truly I tell you, anyone who will not receive the kingdom of God like a little child will never enter it."* The Kingdom of God is a system. Being trained in this system is what guarantees a person's success when they grow up, not only into a Christian individual, but also on the world stage as superior ambassadors of God Almighty.

Here, Jesus is reiterating the fact that operating in the God-system is what makes you superior. However, being trained in how to operate such a system requires absolute faith in the training syllabus itself *(the Bible)*, the author of the Curriculum *(God)* and the person delivering the training *(Parents)*. Now, I need you to thoroughly catch what I am about to say next.

Every training has its rewards – and so also does the word of God, which is the basis of all Christian training. How much of the reward a person gets from the training depends on how much of that training was adequately absorbed. In turn, how much training that is absorbed depends on how much <u>faith</u> or <u>doubt</u> there is within the student receiving the training *(in our case, a child)*. You see, we as parents cannot fully protect our children from the world because they have to grow in it. You cannot also prevent them from growing up because that is just the natural order of life. These two uncontrollable parameters mean that a time is coming when they would stop being a child and by extension, they would stop being retainers.

When this happens, a third uncontrollable event will be in place – you will be unable to fully control what they hear, see, taste and feel. As a result, thoughts will start being formed within them, personal opinions will be formed and so also will ideologies, worldly truths and realities. It is these things which become part of a growing person that builds a conflict within them against: the content of Godly training, the sovereignty of God as the author of the training material, and against the Christian parent, being the one who delivers the training. Effectively, the three main areas in which a person needs to have faith, in order to absorb training the best possible way, start being conflicted against once they grow out of childhood.

Yes, conflict. Conflict, because the worldly syllabus for success conflicts with the biblical basis for success. Conflict, because the author of the worldly syllabus, Satan, is an enemy to the author of our Christian syllabus – God. Conflict, because a Christian parent's approach to raising a child is in conflict with the way the parents of the world consider best to raise children.

As a child however, these conflicts are minimised and therefore, faith is multiplied. A child's faith is simply one that accepts, absorbs and retains the Godly syllabus, Godly author and Godly parent without asking questions. In other words, as a child, it is easier for the trainee *(child)* to fulfil all the three required levels of faith in order to get the best out of training being provided. That's why we need to train up A CHILD not an adult.

You see, good training is one that requires the trainee to do what he is being trained in, as he is being trained in it. This is very true of children – all you have to do is to get a child to "act" in the desired way and they will do it over and over again, no questions asked. It makes training practical, because once the act is repeated it becomes their default act. If you act out praying to be fun, a child will also act it out until it becomes his/her default act. If you act out singing and shouting Hallelujah to a child, it will become their default personality act. If you act out going to church, sharing, loving your spouse, being thankful and appreciative, doing the dishes…. they will become the default personal acts of the child – in other words, a carefully sculptured second nature. On the contrary, a young person or adult if asked to act, as part of a training process, will normally run such requests through their thinking first and attempt to align it to their reasoning, philosophies, ideologies etc. – and sure enough, such thinking processes block training from being received in its wholesomeness.

Train Up: More than Just Training a Child

The equivalent of the phrase *"train up"* equates to *"Chanak,"* which incidentally has more than one meaning, one of which is *"dedication."* In other words, the scripture *"Train up a child in the way he should go...."* Can equally be read as *"Dedicate* a *child in the way he should go...."*

The act of dedication is not something that is done once. The very term "dedicate," implies it has to be done continuously and relentlessly. Dedication is not any ordinary act. It is an act which has an end result in sight. To be dedicated at something means there is an inherent expectation that a certain definite result will be achieved at a certain time in the future insofar as the dedication is continued. Until that expectation is arrived at, dedication has not been completed. What does this mean for parents? It means that parents need to know from the start what they want their training to achieve for their child, so that they simply don't train up a child because everybody else is training theirs in a certain way – otherwise, it is no more training, it has become education.

Another inherent nature of dedication is that it is an act that believes a continuous and relentless action, when applied to a person or thing will cause such a thing or person to become aligned or formed into a certain nature. That belief is anchored on the person or thing being malleable enough to be moulded, remoulded and moulded without losing its strength – and that is exactly the state of a child.

A child's nature, personality, ability, persona, character, strengths, weaknesses etc.; the very being of a child is malleable enough to be bent, straightened, stretched and compressed without losing its strength or quality. Like a rod of iron heated to red hot; it is in this most malleable and yet vulnerable state that it can be transformed from just an ordinary bar of iron into a useful, value added item. And yet, it is still iron in every sense of the word when it cools down – this is the very nature of a child and hence, why it is best to dedicate children to training when indeed they are children. An adult on the other hand is like a cold bar of iron – stiff, not malleable and hard to change, though not impossible.

4

THIS IS **THE WAY** TO GO
(THE CONTENT)

It is important that I stress this here. Even though this chapter deals with some of the core things to train a child in, sight should not be lost of what we discussed in Chapter Two – the methods used to administer the content. Inasmuch as I would have loved to describe the best training method applicable to each content listed here, I recognise that each child and the circumstances around their growth is different. As a result, some of the *"training-up"* methods may be good for some and not for others. In fact in the case of some children, there may well be the need to use several different training methods to achieve the purpose.

There are some qualities which simply need to be an essential part of a person for him to turn out well in life. I beseech you, please don't for one moment, throw your hands in the air and say *"we are imperfect human beings."* Yes, we may be now, but it doesn't equate to remaining the same forever. No, in fact God Himself recognises the possibility of us attaining perfection, so His word says in Matthew 5:48 *"Therefore be perfect, just as your Father in heaven is perfect"*

So, just what should you train your child in? Many things; but before we go into it all, there a few things to keep in mind:

(i)   Firstly, accept the truth that it is not all going to happen in one day or one year, so don't kill the child with pressure and don't derange yourself with frustration. Remember, a child is a *"retainer"* or better put, a voluminous storage tank. S/he may not exhibit what you are training them for right away, but if it has been repeated enough, have faith that it has been soaked and retained in the reliable archives of their minds and beings.

(ii)   Also bear in mind as we talked about in one of the earlier chapters, that some of the contents your child will need training in are such that if you don't practice them yourself, it will be hard for you to train them in it. A man cannot give what he does not have; Acts 3:6 – *"Then Peter said, "Silver and gold I do not have, <u>but what I do have I give you</u>."* It doesn't mean it cannot be taught. It means you have to learn it yourself before training your child in it, or, that you should consider committing your child to someone you trust who has such a grace.

(iii) Finally, remember that a child is a retainer – a hungry sponge of brain, five senses and personality. Do not feel they are limited in their ability to absorb. Let the child define the ultimate limit – 2 Corinthians 5:16 – *"Therefore, from now on, we regard no one according to the flesh...."* If you gauge the absorbing ability of a child by virtue of their size or frailty, you will be short-changing them and doing them more disservice in the end than good.

In no particular order, I will now proceed to list some core qualities, characters and natures that every godly child should be trained in, in order that they can find success in life. I am not saying this is an exhaustive list, because that would be very naïve of me, but I am certain these qualities form the biggest comer-stones with which a successful life can be built. Under each heading, I will attempt to show very succinctly, why such a quality is essential to the future of a child, examples in the Bible and basic ideas on how it can be practically taught to a child. These practical ideas are just guides to start you off finding your own innovative ways of delivering these contents in ways best suited to your child. And I pray the creative power of the Holy Spirit guides you. I believe He will if you ask Him – I did.

Here are three important things to bear in mind when training your children in the ways of God:

(i)   Everything you do has to be deliberate, with a goal behind it.
(ii) Every part of their daily lives and yours is a training opportunity – everything.
(iii) Once taught, the content has to be re-enforced, repeated and grounded before letting go.

God, Christ and the Holy Ghost

Why it's necessary: If your children don't grow up knowing your GOD, they will grow up knowing the god of this world and lose their Christian heritage – somehow the vacuum will be filled one way or another. They will otherwise learn and accept evolution and the baseless philosophy that man is God and that God does not exist. They need to be taught that God is everything and the creator of all.

Examples in the Bible:

(i)   Daniel 11:32 – *"the people who know their God shall be strong and carry out great exploits."*

(ii) Deuteronomy 4:39 – *"Therefore know this day, and consider it in your heart, that the LORD Himself is God in heaven above and on the earth beneath; there is no other."*

(iii) Deuteronomy 11:19 – *"You shall teach them to your children, speaking of them when you sit in your house, when you walk by the way, when you lie down, and when you rise up."*

Practical: It's easiest to point to nature and all its elements and ask your child *"Do you know who made that?"* Point and ask them about trees, the sun, the moon, the rain when it falls. You may be startled at the result, but once they get the hang of things, they will soon be labelling all things as made by God – and that in itself, is truth. You can explain to them that with things like cars, bicycles, computers and phones etc., God showed the picture to a man or woman and it was made. That way, you are preparing them to accept that all good and excellent things come from God. Your child would also have started absorbing the fact that all things are by God, but for some, He designates man to manifest.

Ask them if they know where God lives? Lie down on the

floor with them and close your eyes and ask them to imagine how magnificent the house of God looks, then ask them to paint it – these are all helping to internalise God in them and make Him real to them. Encourage them to say good morning to God when they wake up, just like they say it to Mummy and Daddy *(if they do)* and also good night and invitations to eat at the table. Play a game in the car – you mention a thing and they say whether it was made by God or man (through God's inspiration) and then switch it around. About Jesus, tell them how we were all naughty and God wanted to spank us but Jesus. His son, really liked us and He came to take our place for the spanking etc. As for the rest, I'll allow your imagination to work it out.

The Word of God

Why it's necessary: It teaches them to eventually grow up knowing that there is an unfailing, authoritative reference point to refer to for all their actions, problems and cares in life. If structured well, they will understand that even Mummy and Daddy use it and are subject to its directions. This gives some safety to their future because when they hit any rock or wedge in their life's journey, you are assured that they will seek counsel from the right source – the Bible. Better still, it is reassuring to know, that when they are fully grown and leave home, they have a standard they can live by - perhaps not at all times, but most enough times to keep them safe.

Examples in the Bible:

(i) In Deuteronomy 32:46 the Bible entreats us to teach the word of God to our children as follows: *"and he said to them: "Set your hearts on all the words which I testify among you today, which you shall command your children to be careful to observe—all the words of this law."*

(ii) Joshua 1:8 – *"This Book of the Law shall not depart from your mouth, but you shall meditate in it day and night, that you may observe to do according to all that is written in it. For then you will make your way prosperous, and then you will have good success."*

Practical: The most effective approach I've noted is to refer to the Bible at every opportunity, as the basis for all your actions. Hopefully if you have read stories for them in the past from the Bible, then refer to those stories. Say things like *"I know all the toys are yours, but you should share them with Amy. Do you remember the story of the Good Samaritan we read about the other day? He was a good man wasn't he? Okay, if you want to be like that good man, then you can give some of your toys to Amy"* but don't force them. Follow up and ask them *"Would you like to be like the Good Samaritan?"* Go ahead, even whisper to them *"Do you want to know a secret? If you give some of your toys to Amy, Jesus will be happy with you in heaven and all the angels will clap for you."*

    Yes, it's a bit of work having to exaggerate things to make

them sound fun but the most important thing is that you are hammering the Bible into the child without them even knowing. Say things like *"We have to feed the cat because the Bible says to and if we do, God will be happy with us"* or things like *"I know Jade hit you but the Bible tells us it is better to forgive them than to hit them back and if you forgive them, God will be happy with you."* Carefully crafted approaches like this, helps the child grow up knowing that everything they do calls for a choice between pleasing God and not.

Very soon, they will start coming to you as a parent to ask if certain actions they are contemplating will make God happy or not. Show excitement and tell them you are really happy that they asked first before taking the action, give them the answer, but before that ask them what they think in order to help them start forming their own opinions. Then finally, encourage them to come back if they still aren't sure.

If they make a mistake, don't just scold them; at least ask them if they first thought about whether their action would have made God happy or not. If they claim they thought about it and yet got it wrong, it's okay. The most important thing is that they are developing their ability to divide rightfully between the will of God. You should correct them and encourage them to keep trying. Where they have gone wrong, find a story in the Bible that has a corresponding concept and tell it to them so they can remember in the future.

Hope, Faith, Patience and Never Giving Up

Why it's necessary: I have combined Hope, Patience, Faith and the
virtue of not giving up, because at a tender age, instilling all four is
based on the same premise – the expectation will be fulfilled if you
tarry. Learning to have hope, faith or not giving up will ensure that
children grow up not missing key fulfilments in their destiny journey. God's destiny for them and in general, all good expectations in
life do come to pass, but giving up easily before they come, may cause
them to miss many golden opportunities. Giving up too early also
produces a person who is happy to start *"things"* but characteristically
unconcerned about following them through to completion. For persons with this undeveloped nature, you shouldn't find any surprise
in them giving up on their careers, businesses, marriages, children
etc. God is always on time with His promises, but it is the impatience
of us humans that need be tamed in order that we may always find
God's fulfilled promises in the end.

Examples in the Bible:

(i)   Father Abraham (Genesis 13, 15, 17) waited patiently,
      having faith and hope in God for the birth of Isaac – he
      almost missed him for Ishmael;

(ii) Romans 5:5 – *"Now hope does not disappoint, because the
      love of God has been poured out in our hearts by the Holy
      Spirit who was given to us"*

(iii) Luke 17:6 – *"So the Lord said, "If you have faith as a mus-*

tard seed, you can say to this mulberry tree, 'Be pulled up by the roots and be planted in the sea,' and it would obey you."

Practical: Luckily, there are hundreds of practical ways this can be taught. Once you understand the underlying approach, it is easy to design your own training modules for this. Always find an opportunity to create an artificial delay for something your child is eager to do or have. Multiply their age by two and that's the number of minutes to hold the delay for. It is not a rule of thumb, but it is essential that teaching this principle does not also kill the child's excitement. So if the child is one year old, try achieving with them a patience span of two minutes. Start slowly. For example, you can put a line of his favourite biscuits or sweets in front of him and stop him from rushing on them for the related number of minutes. It won't be easy at first, but you will get there. One of the most important things to factor into the artificial delay is to ensure that the expectation is still achieved. So in our example above, he'll still get the sweets at the end of the artificial delay.

It begins to form within the child's mind that the expectation can still be fulfilled with patience *(or delays).* As they begin to grow up, reinforce this training – cancel an event you planned with them, postpone it once, twice, thrice, then spring up a surprise and make it happen, bigger than originally *planned (just make sure that both parents are in the know what is happening and that both are committed to seeing it through).*

About hope and never giving up, try helping them build a stack of something – boxes or cans or anything. Just when they reach the top, secretly topple it and encourage them not to delay but build it right back up. Do this twice and help them succeed on the third try or fourth or fifth as they grow. Whenever they fail first time at something, always encourage them *"it can be done"* and spur them on immediately to try again. The trick is not to allow time in-between the failure and the restart, because it is in that window of opportunity that the devil gets the chance to speak to us saying *"You failed, it's impossible, you are no good"* etc.

Thankfulness and Gratitude

Why it's necessary: This is a virtue which works both with God and men. An ungrateful heart is never considered worthy of anything more than what they failed to be grateful for.

Examples in the Bible:
(i)   1 Samuel 2: Hannah, a hitherto barren woman, the mother of Samuel, gratefully gives Samuel to God and God rewards her with more children.

(ii)   Jeremiah 30:19 – *"Then out of them shall proceed thanksgiving and the voice of those who make merry; I will mul-*

tiply them, and they shall not diminish; I will also glorify them, and they shall not be small"

(iii) Ephesians 5:20 – *"giving thanks always for all things to God the Father in the name of our Lord Jesus Christ"*

Practical: The surest ways to teach gratitude is to be grateful yourself and to teach a child very early to say *"thank you"* for everything s/he receives. Here's how. When they have something in their hands, stretch your hand as though asking for it and when they give it to you, say *"thank you"* with excitement, clap for them or hug them. Repeat *"thank you"* several times. Now reverse and give them something and encourage them to say *"thank you..* If they haven't started talking yet, say it for them – it will be absorbed for the future.

Another sure way is to make it obvious between both parents. When Daddy receives anything from Mummy, let him say *"thank you"* and vice versa. Natural repetitions like this are very easy for children to absorb. Don't think they are too young to understand – yes, they may not understand it all now, but if the acts are re-enforced now the understanding behind it will be much easier to absorb subsequently. Get them to say thank you to God before eating and after meals. They should also be encouraged to say thank you to people external to the family who give them things.

As they grow in age, you can take it to another level – Daddy can take them out to buy a card or flower for Mummy, but most importantly tell them why they are being encouraged to buy the card or flower for Mummy – Say things to them like *"Mummy has been really nice to you, cooking your food, bathing you, changing your clothes, washing stuff and this is a way to show Mummy that you know she is a nice person and that you love her."* Whether the child is a boy or a girl, ensure that these acts are done both ways – to Mum and to Dad. You don't want the girl growing up thinking gratitude should only be to her Mum and not her Dad otherwise she may have problems in her marriage. At every opportunity you get, ask them if they offered a *"thank you"* to God. As a parent, demonstrate this by examples and get them to join in.

Giving and Compassion

Why it's necessary: Indeed to give is more blessed than to receive. Giving is always a seed that guarantees future harvests. Giving kills selfishness and greed. Giving is a channel through which God's blessings descend into a person's life. Giving serves as a person's memorial before God. Giving assures God that He can entrust you with greater blessings and wealth. Giving destroys poverty and it's mentality outright.

Examples in the Bible: All throughout the Bible – God gave His only son, that we may be saved. Abraham was willing to give his only son Isaac, Solomon sacrificed a thousand bulls to

God, the Good Samaritan had compassion on the wounded stranger, the little boy gave his loaves and fish to feed the thousands.

(i)   2 Corinthians 9:7 – *"So let each one give as he purposes in his heart, not grudgingly or of necessity; for God loves a cheerful giver."*

(ii) Luke 6:38 – *"Give and it will be given to you: good measure, pressed down, shaken together, and running over will be put into your bosom. For with the same measure that you use, it will be measured back to you."*

(iii) Luke 10:33 – *"But a certain Samaritan, as he journeyed, came where he was. And when he saw him, he had compassion"*

Practical: This is one virtue which is best taught in action. In other words, it is more easily learnt by children seeing it done by Mummy or Daddy. However, that is not to say that it cannot be taught. Depending on how old your child is, you can intentionally walk them to someone begging for alms, give him a coin and get him to give alms and then explain to him – God likes us to help those who don't have as much as we are fortunate to have.

Or make a prior arrangement with an orphanage or children's home. Take your child out shopping, explain to him why you are doing it and even get him to decide some of the shopping list, then drive to the orphanage and give. If you can do this just once a year for three years, it is an impression never to be erased.

And here is an even more important one. Always give them money when in church and get them to sow it in the offering bowl. Even better, show them how to offer thanksgiving to God: On any special occasion for example, on their birthday, the birth of a new sibling, etc., take them to church and give them money to give as special offering, explaining to them that God is the one who gives us such special moments and we should thank Him by praying and offerings. This is training that keeps a person in blessings, always.

Where the child is relatively very young, at least start by always asking them for their food. When they give it to you, don't just throw it away – eat it and thank them, of course with excitement. It will begin to build within them, the sense of sharing what is theirs. Teach them to give simple presents to Mum or Dad, even when there are no special occasions. If they go out with Mum, give them some money *(whilst out)* and the freedom of choice to buy something for Daddy and their siblings; and vice versa when they go out with Daddy.

Confidence and Courage

Why it's necessary: If a person says to himself he can achieve something, then yes he can. If he says he cannot, then no matter how you try, he cannot. That's just confidence – it's the belief in self. And it's the key that turns on the ignition. Confidence and courage allows a person to try new things, explore opportunities, think outside the box and take on challenges. It's the vim from within, which gets a person to surmount issues that others will naturally be buried under – but you have to turn it on.

Examples in the Bible:

(i)   Deuteronomy 31:6 – "*Be strong and of good courage, do not fear nor be afraid of them; for the LORD your God, He is the One who goes with you. He will not leave you nor forsake you.*"

(ii) Job 40:23 – "*Indeed the river may rage, Yet he is not disturbed; He is confident, though the Jordan gushes into his mouth*"

Practical: At a tender age, some children may be born with a natural dose of confidence, others may not. The truth is, confidence can be inspired and the way it works is this – since at such an early age children cannot figure out what it takes to "*believe in themselves,*" parents can help by "*believing in the child.*" At such early ages they are still riding on the wings of Mummy and Daddy, and if the parents can show the child that s/he is backed with Daddy and Mummy's belief, they will soon start believing in themselves – and then is born, their confidence. It's like saying to them "*you can borrow and drive in Mummy and Daddy's confidence until you have yours*".

Practically speaking, teaching courage can be equally exciting. You can start as babies, lifting them up in the air *(please be careful)* until they start finding it more fun, than scary. If that happens, that's a good achievement because most children find that scary for a long time. Next, you can start introducing them to random activities or events they have never done before – initially, they tend to be scared. If that happens, offer to do it with them a couple of times until they can do it themselves. Keep re-enforcing the phrase *"It's fun, isn't it?"* and also *"I knew you could do it, you are a brave boy/ girl" (you see, what you continually tell your child he is, he will believe he is, very early in life).* The fundamental idea is to ensure that you are on the lookout for new things for them to try alone or with you.

The objective of all of this is to get to the point, where if you introduce them to something new, they wouldn't hesitate for a minute to contemplate whether they can do it or not – they will just do it. That's the target, and until you get to that point, you really can't stop.

Prayer and Blessings

Why it's necessary: If you are grooming your child to grow up as a responsible Christian, then I really can't stress enough that teaching them to pray is absolutely important – he needs to grow up knowing that God listens to him and God acts, just like the way Mummy and

Daddy listen and act, but better. Blessing on the other hand, is not the same as prayer. Blessing is very simple – it is the transfer of *"a person's own grace"* or the release of a *"prophetic seed"* into the life of a child by someone in rightful spiritual authority over such a child. This could be a parent, guardian, spiritual leader etc. Bear in mind, you cannot bless with what you do not have or if you are not the right spiritual authority.

I feel this is a bit harsh to say, but I must for the sake of the generations that will be moulded through our hands – many parents know how to pray but very little know how to bless. Understand that if you carry a particularly good grace in something, then you don't need to take it to the grave. That will be pure selfishness – it has to be transferred to your children one way or another.

Examples in the Bible: Jesus prayed, the Apostles prayed, Jacob blessed his twelve sons, and Moses blessed the tribes of Israel.

(i) Luke 11:1 – *"Now it came to pass, as He was praying in a certain place, when He ceased, that one of His disciples said to Him, "Lord, teach us to pray, as John also taught his disciples."*

Practical: Prayer and blessings are not the same, but I have chosen to treat them together because the mode of delivery for both is so similar it can be taught as such. I must say however, prayer can really only be taught children by them seeing it in action. Here's what I think really works:

(i)   You need to consciously pray in the presence of your children and don't hold anything back. Kneel down as you normally would if that's what you do; raise your hands like you normally would; travail as you would normally do, but most importantly don't hold anything back.

(ii)   If your child hangs around you, encourage them to also pray. Permit them to also raise their arms in worship, kneel down in submission, travail etc. It may all appear funny in the start, but at least they are catching the art and craft of prayer.

(iii)   Pray with them in the morning and at night before they go to bed. When they are very young, you cannot pray with them so you will need to put your hands on them and pray for them. I started doing this for my first daughter and by the time she was about 16 months old, she would let me pray for her and then she would also stretch her hands to pray for me – and I so gladly encouraged it. Now she prays for Mummy, Daddy, and her little sibling who Mummy is carrying in her womb. It isn't coincidence.

(iv)   Take advantage of every special occasion, to pray with them. Make them understand that every good thing comes from God and just like they would say thank you to Daddy or Mummy for giving them something, they also ought to say thank you to God first. The truth is, every day, there is an opportunity to help us help our children come to *"....God, with thanksgiving in their hearts"* until it becomes an embedded lifestyle.

(v) Finally, I have noticed one of the most effective ways to teach children to be immersed in prayer is to pray as a family, regularly and consistently.

I wouldn't have done justice finishing on prayer without mentioning this: From an early age it is essential that we immerse children in the understanding that God answers prayer, according to His own sovereignty.

Here's what I suggest: Sometimes when your child asks you for something that you know you are happy to get for them, pause. Don't just say *"Okay!"* Instead, tell them *"I don't think I can get it for you on, but I know who can"* he may excitingly ask you *"Who can get it for me, Mum?"* then tell them, *" I am sure God can, if you ask Him. Remember I told you He has everything right?"* – Now then, go out there, maybe a day or two later and get what they asked for. And when you give it to them, re-enforce their growing belief and tell them *"God gave me the money to get it for you son. Don't you think we should pray and thank God for it?"* Of course he's going to jump up and say *"yes,"* What you have to realise is that you have just immersed that child into knowing (i) he can talk to God as he would you (ii) he can have faith in God to deliver (iii) that God indeed does hear and answer prayer and (iv) where his parents are concerned, God is the ultimate source.

Once in a while, don't get them what they prayed for. They may come and ask you why God didn't answer that prayer. Explain to them that God did and that sometimes when we ask for things, God may not give it because it may not be the best for us. I had the opportunity to explain this to a friend's daughter once and this is what I did. I share it here in the hope that it may help you form your own approach.

The little girl *(I will refer to her as Milli)* had a pet cat. I reached in a first-aid box and handed her a bottle of tincture of iodine and then proceeded to explain to her it was very poisonous and that if it entered anybody's mouth, they could die. Scared, she handed the bottle back to me, but I insisted she held on to it for the moment. Then I asked her if she loved her cat very much and if sometimes when she is holding food in her hands, the cat would ask for some. She responded excitingly *"Timmy (the cat) always wants to eat what I have in my hands."* By now my friend was wondering where I was going with the process. Then I asked Milli *"If Timmy saw you holding this bottle and came to you wanting to drink some of the medicine in it, would you give it to her?"* By now she was angrily shaking her head in total disapproval at my suggestion, so I took the bottle of tincture from her, lifted her unto my lap and said to her *"You see, Milli, sometimes when you ask God or*

Daddy something, He may not give it to you because it may hurt you, just like you didn't want to give that medicine to Timmy even though Timmy asked for it. It doesn't mean He doesn't want you to have it, it just means that He loves you so much He doesn't want to give you something that will hurt you, okay. Don't you think that's very nice of God and Daddy?" – Well, what can I say, *"Case closed, mission accomplished,"*

Where blessings are concerned – we are transferring a grace that we are endowed with or have been blessed with. However, there is also such a blessing, called a *"Prophetic Blessing"* which is a grace we do not have, but which we can deposit in the lives of our children because as parents, our voice carries a pro-phetic ability *(through God)* to impact their lives. From time to time it is beneficial that we look at our own lives and list out the graces we have been endowed with freely by God, lay our hands on our children and release such graces upon them too. See, you may find it easy to forgive, exercise patience, be creative, dream, see visions etc. The truth is these things don't come easily to everybody, but insofar as they are excellent graces, nothing stops you from blessing your children with it. Likewise where prophetic graces are concerned, you can bless your children with it. However, I must give this word of warn-ing where prophetic blessings are concerned – don't do it for selfish reasons *(Don't do it merely because you wanted such a grace so badly and never had it so you want your child to have it at all cost)* and don't do it for the sake of competition *(maybe someone's child has such a grace and so you feel your child must have it too)*. Not so, I beg of you, not so.

Whatever blessing you bless your child with, let it be a blessing that will (i) multiply their experience of God and (ii) help them reach their destiny safely. It must not become a burden on them. To end, I want to suggest that every parent should at least be able to learn and bless their children every day with the Aaronic blessing in Numbers 6:

> "The Lord bless you
> And the Lord keep you,
> The Lord make His face to shine upon you
> And the Lord be gracious to you;
> The Lord lift up His countenance to you
> And the Lord grant you peace"

It is the only prayer in the Bible that God Himself crafted and promised that every time it is prayed, His Name shall be upon whoever it is prayed – at least, let God's name be on your child every day.

A Lifetime Reader and Learner

Why it's necessary: Readers will always be leaders. Knowledge *(past, present and future)* has only two places of storage – in books and in men. So, in order to access past, present and future knowledge, it either has to be transmitted from mouth to ear or from book to mind. I will not say the latter is the best, but you will agree it's the form of knowledge storage that lives on even after human knowledge carriers die and pass on.

Examples in the Bible: The Bible referred to Jesus as being very knowledgeable even as a child. In Luke 2, Jesus at the age of twelve attends a feast in Jerusalem with His parents and was later found teaching the teachers of the day. Rabbis marvelled at the depth of His knowledge. He was exceptionally knowledgeable at the age of twelve. Soon after that we never hear about Jesus again until at the age of thirty when He resurfaced again to start His ministry. In-between those two ages, ancient Jewish wisdom teaches that He was intensely being schooled in all manner of knowledge in order to get Him ready for ministry.

(i)   Proverbs 1:5 – *"A wise man will hear and increase learning, And a man of understanding will attain wise counsel"*

(ii) Proverbs 9:9 – *"Give instruction to a wise man, and he will be still wiser; Teach a just man, and he will increase in learning."*

Practical: It is essential to help children from an early age, read widely. Three sources I recommend that are both fun and yet informative are the Bible, encyclopaedias and the Guinness Book of Records. Here's one psychological advantage of reading widely: not many people do so. A lot of children pretty much just read Bible stories and story books. Getting your child to read and be in the know of exciting facts such as from the Encyclopaedia and Guinness Book of Records, makes them *(on most occasions)* the talk centres in school and among their friends because they know some very cool stuff which other children don't know. The effect - it makes them want to know more, but it also raises their confidence.

An added advantage of this is, very early in their lives, you can see which sections of these books they take deeper interests in and therefore where they have a likely tendency to explore later in life. Some newspapers even do children's magazines. If these aren't too expensive, get them a subscription – the mere fact that they can boast of a monthly magazine coming through the post and in their name makes them feel so proud they will really *(not guaranteed)* want to read such educative newspapers *(but of course, you as a parent need to know whether it is educative enough for them or not).*

Finally and most importantly, encourage them to share the things they read with you, and if you are impressed with their findings, do genuinely let them know you are truly impressed and ask them to tell you more. From time to time, ask them what their latest reading discoveries are. If they are reading a story book, let them update you with the story's progress. It might be useful sometimes to do some quick research in some of the areas they are interested in and share with them a few new facts they are likely to find exciting – it's one of the ways you can show them you take their search for wide knowledge seriously and that you are happy to engage with them to explore more. If you notice that they talk to you a lot about dinosaurs, take them to a natural museum to see one. If they talk a lot about houses, arrange with a building engineer friend and take them to a building site. But try and make an effort to tie their reading to real life issues. That way, whatever they read becomes real to them and inspires them to read even further, even wider.

There are some things worth repeating to your child every time you see them reading. It will remain in their mind and will always nag back at them in life, either as an encouragement or a rebuke. Before I list them out, let me just remind you that as the world becomes very technology driven, remember to help your child explore the right channels of reading – don't try to limit them to paperback because believe it or not, paperbacks will soon be extinct. Some of the phrases to use in reinforcing their reading habits are:

(i)   "Readers are always leaders and leaders will always be readers"

(ii)   "Remember Hosea 4:6 'for lack of knowledge my people perish'"

(iii)   "Every time I see you reading, I'm more convinced you'll succeed"

(iv) "You make us really proud with your hunger for knowledge"

(v) "Keep reading until the world reads about you"

Creative Thinking

Why it's necessary: Those who rule in the world now and those who
will be guaranteed any form of success in the future are solution givers
and problem solvers. Irrespective of whether the child is brought
up the God way or not, creativity is one of the greatest ability God
placed in man in order to help him attain dominion – God Himself
created the heavens and the earth so He is the highest creative power
in all realms. It is an ability that trains the mind of a child to identify
problems and create original solutions for them.

It is essential that you accept this before we move forward – that
creativity is God's power within man, enabling him develop original
solutions to problems. The world will always be at the feet of those
who solve problems. Like someone rightly said, *"The world is full of
problems, but short of solution givers."* Problems will always come as
part of life and some of them *(if not most)* come in baffling forms. A
creative thinker is one who thrives in this environment because to
him, a problem is simply the fuel needed to run his creativity engine.

Examples in the Bible: David was exceptionally creative in his
defeat of Goliath, in that instead of using the *"usually accepted
method"* of battling with armour, spears, shield and sword; he

instead deployed a hitherto unknown method – psychological warfare *(when he engaged in a demeaning conversation with Goliath prior to their engagement)* and the use of a sling and stone.

Practical: Here again, I will only attempt to show you the framework within which you can develop your own *"creative"* approaches to training your child. Always pose a problem to your child – it could be anything. Now, tell them what the *"usual"* solution is and then ask them to come up with a different way of solving the problem. If they try or are close *(for starters)*, praise them – the important thing in the early stages is to set them on the path to engaging their creative side. Eventually, they will actually be providing workable solutions – and that's what we are working towards.

Another way you can help them is through *"spatial thinking."* Place a big cardboard paper on the floor, draw a circle in the middle and write something in the middle of the circle. It could be anything – Daddy, TV, school, ice-cream *(basically, random stuff)*. Now make several dots scattered around the middle circle and ask your child to "think about the word in the middle and write beside each of the dots, other words that come to his mind." If they are not at the age they can write yet, help them by writing down in a spatial form, the thoughts that they spew out. Don't disagree with any – that's what creativity is all about.

Two more practical things you can try: Firstly, lie on the floor and blindfold each other. Now start a random story, using any random person or object and after that, both of you take turns to continue with the creation of the unfolding story. It will be helpful if you had a tape recorder tucked away somewhere for this purpose. So, you may start a story say *"Once upon a time, there was a little dog called Pippin"* and your little son or daughter may continue *"and Pippin likes to eat chicken,"* You may continue *"One day Pippin visited a king in a big castle"*… Be as wild and as random as you possibly can be.

Alternatively, you can also buy them a flipchart and get them to paint very random stuff – maybe get them to paint some of the characters from the Bible stories you've told them in the past or to paint any memories of the last outing they had with Mummy or Daddy. The more random it is the better.

Singing

Why it's necessary: Of course the idea is not to teach your child to sing like Pavarotti or Cece & Bebe Winans, but if it is a natural gifting your child possesses and which needs to be developed, then that's a different thing altogether. Singing is one of the most liberating and fulfilling ways to express praise and worship to God almighty – and that is one of the things we were created to do – to worship our God.

Examples in the Bible: King David was a man filled with praise and worship for God, so much that God referred to David as a man after His heart.

(i)   Deuteronomy 31:19 – *"Now therefore, write down this song for yourselves, and teach it to the children of Israel; put it in their mouths..."*

Practical: This is one of those things that a child will more easily pick up by hearing you do it. So get singing with them, but please don't make it look *"routine."* Make it exciting, hold their hands and jump around whilst you sing. There are wonderful Christian rhymes and songs for children on YouTube and all over the internet. In fact you can even use singing to God as a way of developing your child's creativity – say for example they get a new toy, you can ask them *"Do you want to say thank you to God or Jesus for giving you this beautiful toy?"* Chances are they are likely to say yes. If they do, ask them further *"I think Jesus would really like it if you sang him a "thank-you" song... Do you know any thank you song you want to sing for Him?"* If they answer in the affirmative, it doesn't matter which song they choose to sing, encourage them and sing along – the most important thing is that it is being registered in their system that they are singing to give thanks – and that's the objective, really. If they don't know any thank-you song, it's still an excellent opportunity – help them formulate a new song. Ask them to sing it anyhow and assure them that the most important thing is that Jesus will be happy to hear them sing. Believe me some of the songs may be hilarious *(please don't laugh)*, and some may be downright silly – but you are forming in them, confidence, creativity and most importantly a heart for thanksgiving.

The best practical advice I can give on this is: whether an occasion demands it or not, sing praises and worship to God and encourage them to join in. Make it theatrical so that it looks more exciting for the kids to join in. When they ask and even when they don't ask, tell them *(and re-enforce it to them every time they see you singing),* that the reason you are praising God is because: He is God, or because He has given everybody in the family food to eat, or because He has made everybody in the family healthy and not ill. Connecting children to every-day reasons for singing to God will start establishing in them the understanding that they really don't need any exceptional reason to worship or praise God Almighty – and that's what touches the heart of God. Do it as often as you possibly can until you notice it becomes a natural part of their lives.

Finally, from time to time, as the family is seated together, ask what your child's favourite song is, or what new songs he has learnt recently and let the whole family sing along with him. Or if he has attempted in the past to create his own *"thank-you" song* for Jesus and this was recorded, play it back and let the whole family savour it and applaud him. Let the encouragement sound like *"Oh wow! Jesus will be really happy with that song.*" You have not only shown the child you believe in them, you have also given them a reason to praise or worship God some more – and in a very creative way. It is deliberate, it is charted.

Honesty and Truthfulness

Why it's necessary: Honesty and truth are the only basis for trust. It doesn't matter whether you are trying to gain the trust of God or man; the two levels on which it will be determined are whether you are honest and truthful.

These are virtues that will defend you at all times without having to work so hard yourself. They are virtues that will cause unknown men to be comfortable enough to entrust you with secrets and deep revelations you would otherwise never know. These are virtues that let a man, whether young or old, have a peaceful sleep at night without reason for fear or dread. You need to understand that when your children grow up, it is to their and your advantage, that they be successful in business or whatever it is that they do – and they cannot succeed in anything if nobody will trust them.

Examples in the Bible: Gehazi was dishonest and untruthful to the prophet Elisha and as a result, not only did he lose an opportunity to receive the anointing upon Elisha, but he also received a curse on himself and on all his descendants (2 Kings 5)

(i)   Proverbs 12:19 – *"The truthful lip shall be established for-ever, But a lying tongue is but for a moment."*

(ii)   Proverbs 12:22 – *"Lying lips are an abomination to the LORD, But those who deal truthfully are His delight"*

(iii) Proverbs 12:19 – *"The truthful lip shall be established for-ever, But a lying tongue is but for a moment"*

Practical: Here is a very powerful psychological tool to use in helping your children. When you notice they have lied to you or have been dishonest – don't let them know immedi-ately you've found them out. If you told them immediately, they may use that as a yardstick to measure your reactions to their dishonesty; then they will go ahead and test the bound-aries, If they do it again and get no reaction from you, they will assume *(and maybe rightly so)* that you did not find out or that you could never find out. My suggestion would be to wait for at least two days and subsequently when they are in need of something very important, break the news to them. Let them know you knew about their dishonesty all along and let them know their action is a just basis for you to deny them what they currently need from you. Explain to them that firstly, you never expected that from them and that if they continue like that, they will end up hurting and losing all the wonderful people around them.

See, delaying telling them that you knew all along cre-ates the ever lingering question in their minds: *"Okay, I know*

Mummy/Daddy is acting normally, but does s/he know all the other things I have been trying to hide?" This ever present prodding question will always show up on their mental screen any time they think about being dishonest or lying. You need to make them understand nobody likes a dishonest person and God is very unhappy with people like that. Tell them the Bible story of Gehazi, the servant of Elisha *(which paints a picture of the repercussion of dishonesty in 2 Kings 5).*

That having been said, it is essential that all training should have a positive impact and not leave the child unnecessarily isolated. For that matter I also suggest that you try and enquire from your child, why he acted in the dishonest manner – there may have been an underlying reason needing dealing with. Whatever the case, explain to him no matter how hard the truth is, it must always be told. Assure him you will not be angry for him telling you the truth, but on the contrary, you'll be happier he told you the truth at all times.

A good practical alternative is to have an *"honest truth box"* for Mummy and Daddy into which your child can scribble on a piece of paper and drop in, and which the parents can empty and read from time to time. The box will be for issues the child would have loved to talk to both of you about but feels bad, embarrassed or upset about. I am sure you will find your own way of doing this, but the most important thing is that you are still consciously creating an avenue that will make your child feel comfortably compelled to communicate the truth no matter how heavy.

You could also have a *"dawn talk time"* for your children – an agreed timeframe say 4am – 6am within which if they knock on your bedroom door to tell you something, they have a guarantee that you will not scold them, fight them, be angry with them etc. *(also applies to the honest-truth-box)*, but that you will listen to them and reason them out. These are essential systems that need to be in place – it will save everybody a lot of hidden troubles.

Some parents may go as far as actually *"testing"* the integrity of their children. There are good ways and bad ways of doing this, but this book unfortunately is not the volume to elaborate on that. Do bear in mind however that if this backfires, your child may feel *"unjustifiably distrusted"* – and that, my friends, is a hard net to get out of – because the ripple effect of that is that they would start being secretive and isolated.

Making Decisions and No Excuses

Why it's necessary: Being able to make decisions and acting on them can be the difference between losing an opportunity or getting the best out of it – and some opportunities don't show up twice. Making decisions and living with it is one of the core qualities of leadership and a proof of one's mental stability. In this world people feel more secure around those who are not overly erratic in their decision making and actions. Being able to make decisions and own them is proof of one's ability to take responsibility for one's actions and hence exercise maturity. The truth about this last point is that not only God, but men, will never commit certain truths and opportunities to immature or shaky persons.

Examples in the Bible: **Luke** 9:62 – *"But Jesus said to him, 'No one, having put his hand to the plough, and looking back, is fit for the kingdom of God.'"*

Practical: Training your child in decision making, is essentially training them to be able to create choices, then choosing right; or where choices already exist, to simply choose right. It is also about measuring choices against each other and selecting which choice provides the best lasting benefits or the least recurring losses. The important things to bear in mind are:

(i)   Always bring your child to a place where a choice has to be made between options. Explain to them what the benefits and drawbacks are likely to be if they made the right or wrong choices respectively.

(ii)   Tell them to ask any questions they feel is necessary to help them make a correct decision between the choices *(oblige but don't tell the answer)* – it will teach them that the more quality information they have, the greater the chances of making the right decision.

(iii) Get them to make the decision

(iv) If they get it right, applaud them and if they don't, encourage them – letting them know that it is okay to get it wrong once in a while, but the important thing is to try not to make the same wrong decision again. *(This ensures that anytime they get it wrong, they take note and learn from their mistake)*

(v) You could even make it rewarding by offering a prize for making three correct decisions in a row. This way you are re-enforcing the learning, that decision making is rewarding.

The reason for describing the above framework is so you can design your own detailed approach to teaching decision-making. But, believe me opportunities abound in your interaction with your children every day, as long as you are intentionally looking out for it.

Here is a simple one you will come across pretty much every day: Say you come to a junction or three junctions away from home *(preferably if you are driving)*, you can ask your child to decide which junction to take home. Stop the car and explain that if he makes the right decision you will both get home in time to catch a good movie, grabbing some of his favourite biscuits or ice-cream on the way. If he gets it wrong, you will get lost and if you do get home, there will be no bonuses. Stick to the deal, no softie softie. Allow them to ask any questions they want and once done, let them make a decision – no changes allowed subsequently.

Here is another good example – Let's assume you agreed to get your child a present on his birthday *(hopefully it's not supposed to be a surprise)*. Drive him to the shop and ask for two or three choices of what he wants. One of the rules is this – items paid for cannot be returned. One excellent rule to factor in is to give the child as much time to think carefully about the decision to make. It is important they learn that decisions once made, should be committed to, and hence every effort and time needed to get it right first time is worth making.

Healthy Lifestyle

Why it's necessary: Our health is actually one of the very few areas of our lives that we do have some form of control over. Think about it – we can control our diet, our bodily and mental fitness and as a result, our overall fitness for purpose. It is no secret that improving your physical fitness through activity *(and there are many forms of activity, not necessarily only the gym)* does improve the flow of blood to the brain and for that matter, improves psychological and general wellbeing.

Maybe, even looking beyond just the mental effect, physically fit people generally tend to have a better resistance to diseases, fatigue and stress; and that can translate into a lot of excellent benefits such as a more lively and confident personality and a better intimate lifestyle during marriage. Surely these are all good things that could be of excellent benefit to your child – any child for that matter.

Examples in the Bible: In both 1 Samuel 2:26 and Luke 2:52 we read about how Samuel and Jesus as children, grew in "stature" signifying their fitness. It must have been very important to God, to be included with other qualities, such as wisdom and favour.

Practical: The physical development of our children, matter equally as much as their spiritual development – after all, a healthy spirit cannot live within a weak body. Let's get them out to play, take them to the beach and swim together, run with them, race with them, climb a tree after them, engage them with nature and encourage them to eat healthily too. The world is changing rapidly. It is daily becoming an E-world *(an electronic world),* Children today find it easier to just sit in front of the TV, spend hours on the computer, eat fast food and play computer games instead of being outside, enjoying nature. It only means we, as parents need to lead the way and put in a greater effort in getting children to be physically more engaged.

Personally, I think enrolling them into some form of physical evening activity will do them a lot of good. But it must be an activity or sport, that doesn't only expend their energy, but one from which they can also draw some quality lessons. For example, soccer, basketball or other team sports have the added advantage of inculcating in them, team-spirit. Some individual sports do help with instilling the ability to focus and in some cases, discipline. Board games will not expend their energy nor help them gain physical fitness, but it does provide a mental equivalent of fitness. I am not saying it shouldn't be encouraged, but the focus here is for the improvement of their physical stature. I should also add that how a person feels about themself has the greatest positive or negative impact on their confidence.

Timeliness

Why it's necessary: Time indeed they say is money – that's the worldly view of time. From the Biblical perspective, it says – "there is a time and a season for everything under the sun…" What many Christians fail to realise is that time is also a vehicle of blessings. God is an on-time God and being created in His nature requires that we be the same. Both in the physical and spiritual worlds, there are seasons and times for different opportunities and blessings. Time is like a capsule in which are various blessings and opportunities. Missing a particular timing means missing the opportunities and blessings that were embedded in that time cloud. You cannot recover it back and sadly but truthfully, some of those opportunities and blessings will never come back either – never.

Personally, I believe being a timely person is a singularly very advantageous characteristic that should not be exchanged or lost for anything. One's consistent ability to be on time shows that they can be relied upon, they are disciplined, they are consistent and they have respect for other people. In fact, very highly successful people use a person's attitude to time as a gauge of their attitude to wealth, responsibility or anything else that may be committed into their care, including secrets.

Examples in the Bible: **Ecclesiastes 3:** *"there is a time and season for everything that is done on the earth"*. This means that "time" is the platform on which mankind can synchronise his/her engagement with God's agenda on the earth. All through the Old Testament, you will see that angels appeared to those they were sent to at very specific times of the day and in specific seasons.

Practical: Here again, being on time as parents is one of the fastest ways to train your children in being timely. There are however, other approaches that work and here too, you are allowed to use your imaginations as wildly as possible. I will again lay down the framework within which you can design your own training:

(i)   Buy your child a new wrist watch *(most boys love digital sports watches)*, then schedule an appointment with your child, and let them know you want to see if they will be on time. *(Give it a competitive tone – most children love an opportunity to prove themselves)*. Obviously this training cannot be done until the child is at an age where they can be taught the clock and its readings. Now, the scheduled appointment could be anything you can imagine, but to start you off here are a few silly but workable examples (i) You could ask them to meet you at the gate of the house at exactly 17:00 pm when you arrive from work. The trick with this however is, you may have to get there earlier to be sure that they made it there on time. (ii) You can ask them to wake you up on Saturday morning at exactly 07:32 am or (iii) you can get them to call you at work at exactly 14:41 pm *(any other time will do)* using Mummy's or Daddy's phone *(or the house phone if there's one)*. The idea I am trying to portray here is that the appointment could take any form and it doesn't necessarily have to involve a physical meeting as long as it is something that allows you to verify their real time involvement at the time assigned. The more varied the nature of the appointments, the greater the chances your child will perceive the need to exercise timeliness in all areas of life's engagement – not only when a physical meeting is involved.

(ii)   Make sure that as part of the scheduling, an incentive is promised – it doesn't need to be a new present; it could well be something they have already asked for, but whose fulfilment is now made contingent on their successful execution of *"timeliness."* Personally, I prefer parents to use a completely new incentive with a further condition that it will be won if their timeliness test is passed and lost if not. Sometimes the idea of having to lose a thing can serve as a much stronger incentive than gaining it.

(iii) Finally, if they pass the test, appreciate them and tell them how proud you are of them and how certain you are, that they will pass subsequent tests. If they didn't pass, well, the fact that they lost a rewarding treat will be their inspiration to get it right next time; but do still tell them that as hard as we try, sometimes we may still get it wrong although you are hopeful that they will get it right next time. If you feel their dejection may degenerate into some form of isolation, you can subtly organise another test soon after, offering the same prize.

As your child grows older, you could increase the responsibility that comes with failing timeliness training. For example, you can ask your child of say 7 years to be the one to wake everybody up next Sunday morning at 06:00 am, making them aware if the family doesn't wake up at the agreed time, everybody will be late for church and vice versa. But of course with such increasing responsibility should come a sizeable treat.

This training is one that will be on-going until such a time as you are convinced that your child has attained consistency in the execution of timeliness.

Loyalty

Why it's necessary: Loyalty is a rare attribute in our modern world. I often define it as an *unwavering faithfulness*. It is the quality of the highest nobility – a quality that not only brings ordinary men into the presence of kings, but keeps them there.

No king ever surrounds himself with people whose loyalties can waver or be questioned. Loyalty is the quality in a person that makes them see past the weaknesses of others and stick with them until their destiny is accomplished. Loyalty is the quality that makes you the last man standing behind a friend, a brother or a leader when everybody else has turned around and gone. Loyalty is that quality that keeps you committed to the person you committed to first and foremost even though there were chances and opportunities to switch sides.

Loyalty is the quality that segregates noble men from ordinary men. But most important of all, it is the quality that is needed to sustain every relationship that needs to last you for a lifetime – that is why it is a crucial quality in marriage, our walk with God, business, lifelong friends and family.

Examples in the Bible:

(i)   1 Chronicles 28:9 *"As for you, my son Solomon, know the God of your father, and serve Him with a loyal heart and with a willing mind; for the LORD searches all hearts and understands all the intent of the thoughts. If you seek Him, He will be found by you; but if you forsake Him, He will cast you off forever."*

(ii) 2 Kings 2: We read the story of Elisha's loyalty to Elijah which was crowned at the end, by a double portion of Elijah's anointing falling upon Elisha – *"And it came to pass, when the Lord was about to take up Elijah into heaven by a whirlwind, that Elijah went with Elisha from Gilgal"*

Practical: Loyalty is a somewhat difficult thing to teach. When my father taught it to my younger brother and I, we didn't even know he was teaching it until many years later when I was fully grown and independent; his words never ceased ringing in my ears. I was taught *"loyalty"* through our family barber. In a neighbourhood we once lived as kids, was a barber we all *(my Dad, younger brother and I)* visited for our bi-weekly haircuts. Even after we moved from the community, my Dad would still drive us over a long distance to have our hair trimmed at the same barbers. Any time we questioned him, he would reply

"The devil you know is always better than the angel you don't know." Then he would always proceed to add – *In life, always try to be loyal to the people you started off with – it always pays in the long run."*

But I must confess I also learnt this from his working life: My Dad was a building technologist and he had his own set of builders and workmen he used for all his projects. He hardly brought in any new workmen – we witnessed first-hand how his loyalty to them was reciprocated by their loyalty to him. As a result, my brother and I experienced loyalty from two lenses – on the one hand, we were taught it and on the other hand we saw Daddy use it in practice. Practically speaking, apart from demonstrating loyalty to your own children, it is also possible to reinforce the teaching by making the obvious, even more obvious in the context of loyalty:

(i)   Ask your child if they've noticed that as a family you mostly go to one supermarket or market or church or hospital etc.

(ii)   Ask them if they've also noticed that there are also oth-er alternatives available. If they can't see the alternatives, show them.

(iii) Now ask them if they've ever wondered why you or the family as a whole do not use the alternatives. *(Assuming*

they haven't already asked you why the alternatives have
not been used until now).

(iv)   Now explain to them, that it all comes down to the prin-
       ciple of loyalty.

(v)   Now from time to time, select the obvious loyal occur-
       rences and use them to demonstrate the principle of loy-
       alty. An even more real example is to show them how
       loyalty has been one of the reasons without which Mum-
       my would not have been still married to Daddy and vice
       versa.

Excellence

Why it's necessary: Like the writer in the book of Proverbs 22:9 says:
"Do you see a man who <u>excels</u> in his work? He will stand before kings;
he will not stand before unknown men." So you see, many men may be
doing the same work, but it is the man who shows *"excellence"* in his,
who will differentiate between his elevation into kingship or being
lumped together with ordinary men of mediocrity.

Excellence is the extra effort that makes one stand out. In the
world we live in, competition is getting stiffer and ruthless at all levels
and in all spheres of life – the only way to consistently remain ahead
of the competition is to be excellent in everything. This means that
excellence has to become one's natural flare. There is no other way;

and for parents, the choice is really yours from the start, whether you set up your child to end up on the kingship list or in the companion of ordinary men. The allegation must never be levelled against a child saying *"S/he ended her/himself in that lowly life"* because the question God will ask is *"Did you train him/her in the way to go, so when s/he grows up, s/he can walk in the company of kings?"* – The child will grow and end up in the path s/he was trained to walk in. It's that simple, yet that possible.

Examples in the Bible:

(i)   In 1 Samuel 16, David, a very young boy, is recommended as an excellent player of the harp to King Saul and therefore was brought into the palace for the first time. There were many harp players of the era but David is immediately recommended because of his excellence.

(ii)   Proverbs 22:9 emphasises *"Do you see a man who excels in his work? He will stand before kings; he will not stand before unknown men."*

(iii)   Finally, in the book of Matthew 5:48, the Bible expressly tells *us "Therefore you shall be perfect, just as your Father in heaven is perfect."*

Practical: Everything a child does every day of their life is a tool for teaching excellence until excellence is exhibited in everything they do *(or at least, most things).* At a very early age excellence can equate to exceptional orderliness. It is this exceptional orderliness that forms the basis of excellence when growing up. In order to teach this (i) you must keep an eye open to spot every disorder exhibited by your child and (ii) you must consistently *(and I do mean consistently)* and immediately correct the child to convert a disorder or imperfection into order and perfection. Do accept this before we move on – there is nothing wrong with grooming your child to be a perfectionist; Matthew 5:48 says *"Be perfect, therefore, as your heavenly Father is perfect."*

Where a child finishes playing and leaves toys around, get him to pack them up into its box – and neatly too. Where he wakes up in the morning and just guns for the TV, get him back to lay the bed – and neatly too. Where he has finished eating and leaves the dishes in a mess, let him do his dishes – and neatly too. Where he is done having a bath, let everything be restored to order – and neatly too. It is these minor reminders and interventions that become a daily natural part of their lives until they learn to accept that being ordered and neat in all spheres of their living is as naturally necessary as eating breakfast. All this having been said, parents need to bear in mind that the child is in a home, not a military barracks. You do need to find a balance between what is training and what is a military drilling regiment. The latter will backfire.

5

IT'S ALL **ABOUT** THE **CHILD**

Many times in the process of raising, training or bringing up a child, one has the tendency *(unconsciously most times)* to direct the child in a path that does not wholly and singularly serve the interest of the child. More often than not it is never intentional, but all the same it may arise as a result of one or a combination of any number of the following:

(i) You feel that as a parent you know all that's right for the child, when in fact you may probably be lacking.

(ii) There is something missing in your life which you wish you had as a child or achieved as an adult, and you now feel your child must have irrespective of whether it is the right thing for the child or not.

(iii) You probably simply don't know what the child needs or whether he needs it at all.

(iv) Perhaps out of a subtle jealousy or envy, that someone's child has a particular ability, character or thing you feel your child should have too.

(v) Family, friends, other people may have said it, suggested it, hinted it, talked about it and you therefore feel obliged to implement it in your child.

I can understand any of these issues could make us feel a bit guilty, but please don't. The most important reason you are reading this book is because you want to get it right for your child *(or children)* – and that, my friend, is love in action.

There are many things that have been discussed in this book, but it would be a shame if all of it was implemented on the basis of what the parent wants as opposed to what the child really needs. Remember what the scripture says again in Proverbs 22:6. It says: *"Train up a child in the way __HE__ should go and when he is old he will not depart from it."*

It is not the way Daddy wants him to go, neither is it the way Mummy wants him to go. It is not the way teachers want him to go, neither is it the way neighbours and family want him to go. It is the way HE should go.

Of course this chapter is not as detailed as a textbook and yet as simplistic as it may appear to be. I am hopeful that it will outline the core actions and processes to consider in determining how to lead your child in *"HIS"* or *"HER"* way.

More often than not in life we tend to be overly obsessed with doing what we can to correct our weaknesses to the effect that we ignore reinforcing our strengths. In raising children to be success-ful, impactful and God fearing, I implore your efforts to focus more on identifying a child's positives and helping him/her to walk the path that makes the most optimal use of those positives. Believe you me, no man was created by God with more negatives than positives. In fact it is only through our human lenses that we see anything as a negative – to God, all aspects of every created being is *"a perfect work."* There are no negatives.

Here is a very obvious truth – in Proverbs 22:29: *"Do you see a man who excels in **HIS** work? He will stand before kings; He will not stand before unknown men."* Growing into becoming impactful, great and fulfilling in life is not primarily to do entirely with the wealth of the parents, the neighbourhood lived in or any of the aesthetics – s/he can grow to become such a woman or man if and only if s/he excels in HIS work or HER work – not any other person's work. In fact the word "work" there more closely relates to "abilities" hence the verse can more appropriately be read as *""Do you see a man who excels in **HIS** abilities?...."* Now here is the exciting bit: It is "HIS" ability because it is very personal to that child. He is the only one in the entire universe that God has endowed with that one ability or combinations of abilities to make him *(or her)* the perfect *(and only)* candidate to excel in a particular thing, in a particular way.

I tend to say to people, if you would begin to look at your child's abilities, both the ones we call positives and negatives and consider them altogether as a whole and not as individual components, it shouldn't be hard to figure out the exact picture of how they were created by God to function optimally in the world; both to the benefit of the world and the glory of God. Here is the thing: The way your child's body parts are formed, her peculiar reaction to different things around her, his relation to you and other humans – every little thing about your child is unique. It is God revealing to you a roadmap of *"the way in which HE should go...."*

I have listed below some helpful areas to thoroughly consider in determining how to train your child such that s/he turns out walking on "HIS" way, and not your way or any other person's way. It is my prayer that as you engage in these, the Holy Spirit will open your eyes into even more deeper revelations of which path to lead your child on. Clearly, what I am trying to do here is to explain this to you: You see, every child was individually engineered by God, to make impact by walking in a specific path of life. As long as he walks in that peculiar path, he will do excellently well. If he walks in any other path – life for him, becomes a waste, in fact, death. We will, in this chapter, attempt to see how a clear picture of HIS path, can be located. Proverbs 14:12 says: *"There is a way that seems right to a man, but its end is the way of death."*

Seek God's Revelation and Direction

I couldn't stress this more – God, through His Holy Spirit, is still in the business of answering prayers. Your child, when s/he is born, has their whole life ahead of them and whether they do well on the journey of life has everything to do with which route they start the journey on. Let me try and explain it this way: You may be travelling from location A in order to arrive at destinations B, C and D. To do this, you may need to walk, use a car, an aeroplane, and a train for each leg of the journeys. This is exactly how the life journey of your child is like. In order for your child to arrive at each destiny-milestone on time, it is important to arrange the journeys by train, foot, car and air in the most optimum order so that neither the departure times, interchange times nor arrival times are missed. If any are missed, that child isn't going to make his/her appointment with destiny.

However, there is just one little problem – as a parent *(and figuratively speaking)* (i) you won't know beforehand, if the plane will take off safely, have problems in mid-air, have a terrorist attack on board or a faulty landing on arrival (ii) you wouldn't know beforehand, if the car journey might meet an accident on the way, or that there may be a road block due to an unscheduled emergency maintenance or a traffic hold up due to a presidential motorcade etc. (iii) you won't know beforehand, if the walking part of the journey may meet with an unexpected heavy downpour of rain, a sprained ankle, an upset stomach, etc. I think you get the point by now. All I am trying to say is that the only one who, at this very moment, lives in the past, present and future all at once is God. As humans, our limitations where our children are concerned is this – we have only lived in a part of their past, a part of their present and none of their future – God made, lives and knows all three, fully. If you ask me, this is good enough reason to seek God, to speak to us through His Holy Spirit where our children's destiny journey is concerned. And He will.

I say this from the personal experience of God's wonderful grace – each time my children have been born, I have sought God and He has spoken to me very audibly about their future. On each occasion I wanted that voice of God to echo throughout their lives, so I have tried to enshrine it as a living memorial in their names. That way, each time I mention their names, I remind myself of the voice of God concerning them, individually.

If you will talk to God concerning your child's destiny journey, He will speak. Consider very sombrely the words of John 16:13 *"However, when He, the Spirit of truth, has come, He will guide you into all truth; for He will not speak on His own authority, but whatever He hears He will speak; and He will tell you things to come"* When you know the truth of God concerning your child, you will know exactly what path to lead them on irrespective of what people may think.

Let me share with you a very vivid Biblical example: in Genesis 25:23, God spoke directly to Rebekah and said *"...And the older shall serve the younger..."* so all through the growing life of Jacob *(people may call him all sorts of names)* Rebekah understood that his path in life was to be the head and not the tail. As a result, when Isaac was about to give the blessing of the head to Esau and the tail to Jacob, she immediately re-engineered the path of Jacob's destiny to ensure that he received the blessing of the head, not the tail. By so doing, she ensured that Jacob's destiny was fulfilled, in accordance to the will of God in Genesis 25. It is for this reason that when Jacob told Rebekah he was scared he may end up attracting a curse instead of a blessing, Rebekah boldly said to him in Genesis 27:13 *"...my son, let your curse be upon me..."* – because she knew all too well, there was never going to be a curse. Indeed, never again did we hear in scripture that a curse as a result of their actions ever came on Rebekah or Jacob.

In Judges 13: 12-14, Samson's parents seek directly from God, what exactly were to be the rules concerning their child yet to be born: *"Manoah said, "Now let Your words come to pass! What will be the boy's rule of life, and his work?" So the Angel of the Lord said to Manoah, "Of all that I said to the woman let her be careful. She may not eat anything that comes from the vine, nor may she drink wine or similar drink, nor eat anything unclean. All that I commanded her let her observe."* Judges 13:8 – *"Then Manoah prayed to the LORD, and said, "O my Lord, please let the Man of God whom You sent come to us again and teach us what we shall do for the child who will be born."*

Engagement, Repetition, Reactions

It is of paramount essence to engage a child in multiple activities and there is no limit whatsoever to the scope of this. Practically speaking, it should as much as possible involve all major spheres of life. Engage them with nature, technology, domestic activities, sports, humans, religious activities. But most importantly, you should be looking to find out which things they take an immediate, focused, intense or repetitive liking to. So, for example, look out for a child's reaction to people – some children will turn out just naturally friendlier than others and that tells you they have a natural tendency to be a "people-person" – please stop making plans to lead them into a path that functions best in isolation – it is not in their God-given nature. You may find a boy who has an extraordinary fascination with his Mum only when she is baking – please don't make plans to force him to like computer games and Ipads like his other siblings – it is not in his God-given nature.

I am not by any means saying that whatever a child gets attracted to first time is what his or her calling is. No. It takes a combination of things to figure that out, but I am suggesting that you consider the intensity and repetition with which they engage in particular areas of life – it will help you start narrowing down where their natural God-given instincts are headed.

Start Recognising their Instinctive Natures

Every child has some natural characteristics they are stronger in than others. It's just the way God has wired them, in order that they are perfect for their peculiar purposes in life – they should not be ignored.

You see, the way God works is that He designs a purpose for man, then wires him in a way that makes him perfect to fulfil that purpose. Exodus 9:16 – *"But indeed for this purpose I have raised you up, that I may show My power in you, and that My name may be declared in all the earth."* It is more or less like *(I like using this example)* comparing an electric carpet hoover and a hairdryer. In truth, the core components in the two appliances are the same, but the hairdryer can never, in a million years function as the carpet hoover – simply because of the way they have been wired. They have the same components, same manufacturer, same brand, same costs, but different uses – because of different wirings.

See, when a manufacturer creates a product, he expects that the most optimal use will be made of that product as long as it is operated or utilised according to the operational manual. The operational manual always comes enclosed in the product, <u>not without it</u>. God's will for a person is usually partly embedded in a person's nature when they are born – it is therefore wisdom, when raising a child, to look at and within their natures, to have a fairer idea of how they were intended in heaven to function on earth. It is only by raising a person to function in harmony with God's uniqueness within them that they can rise to the fullness or at least close to the fullness of their potentials. In Matthew 6:10, we read "….*Your will be done on earth as it is in heaven*." In other words, if you are raising a child outside of the will of God partly hidden in their natures, then you are raising them without the embedded operational manual they came with – and God's glory cannot be fully made manifest in them.

So, to reiterate, consider thoroughly their natures –Do they like talking instinctively? *(Does that mean they are naturally wired for oratory?)*; Do they naturally have a strong personality? *(Does that mean they are naturally wired for leadership or discipline?)*; Do they naturally come across as perceptive and keen observers? *(Does that mean they are naturally wired for sciences or deep thinking?)*; Do they naturally come across as nature-loving? *(Does that mean they are naturally wired for arts or the more natural elements of life?)*. Are they instinctively restless, always easily bored and searching for new things to be engaged in? *(Does that mean they are naturally wired for exploration and philosophical quests?)*. Recognize their intuitive natures – they hold clues.

> Romans 11:24 *"For if you were cut out of the olive tree which is wild by nature, and were grafted contrary to nature into a cultivated olive tree, how much more will these, who are natural branches, be grafted into their own olive tree?"* Also consider this scripture in Romans 1:19 – *"because what may be known of God is manifest in them, for God has shown it to them."*

Absorption: Hearing, Touching or Sight

If you are already a parent, you'll probably know this and if you are yet to be, then all the better. Some children learn a lot effortlessly by hearing, others more effectively by observation *(sight)* and yet still there may be some who absorb the most by actually doing *(engaging, touching or feeling)*.

Knowing what the best absorption method is for your child will help two things. Firstly, it will help you in administering training to your child in the format that is the most absorbable. Take for example a child who is being taught music, whose absorption ability through hearing is far more pronounced than through sight. For such a child, it is easiest to teach them how to master musical notes *(on whatever instruments)* through hearing rather than through reading *(truth is, even though it is traditionally taught through reading, it can be equally taught through hearing)*. In the recent advent of audio books as well as readable books (eBooks or paper), it is now possible to encourage a child to read in the most effectively absorbable way.

Quite apart from discovering the most effective mode by which a child absorbs training, this knowledge also gives a further indication of what the individual child is most likely wired for. A child whose absorption affinity is skewed towards touching or physical engagement is obviously likely to do well in those aspects of life that require physical engagement or mechanics; whereas on the other hand, a child with a tendency to absorb through observation *(sight)*, is likely better wired for those aspects of life that require keen observation, perception, mental concentration, attention to detail, artistry, creativity etc. For children with an exceptionally keen hearing absorption rate, it is very likely their wiring leans them to aspects of life closely related to communication; thorough understanding and most importantly, that require more listening than talking.

A Fun Journey of Professions and Vocations

I am an ardent proponent of living life practically and where children are concerned, even more so. I am being careful in what I write in this section primarily because, the intention of this book is not to trample on the beliefs or systems that have worked in the upbringing of some parents, which may very well work for their children too. Not everybody in adult life may have turned out to be what they wanted to be when they were children, but then again, some people have turned out in adult life doing exactly what they were in love with when they were children. The thing is, we all, as children fall in love with certain vocations or professions than others. But of course, a child will only express a liking in what they have been exposed to and if it is exciting enough, they will get absorbed in it heart, soul and with total "faith." Every child will come to that point in their growing up, so here are the two most important things I have to say:

(i)   In order that you do not skew their choices or limit their opportunities, I strongly suggest that if you ever talk to your child about vocations and professions, then without preju- dice, tell, them about as many professions as they can han- dle, and I would add, especially emphasising those that align with (i) their natural instincts which you may have observed (ii) the voice of God concerning them and (iii) their best senses of knowledge absorption etc.

(ii)   Secondly, I strongly advise this next point, because it turns childish desires into experiences real enough to transcend past fantasies. If you have managed to substantively narrow down vocations which your child seems enthused about to say between three and five, *(obviously, when s/he is at the appropriate age)* then do this: Diligently locate people you know, who work in those particular fields of interest. If pos- sible, arrange whole day outings for your child, for each vo- cation of interest so he can experience a real work environ- ment in real-time, with real people. This kind of experiences can either transform their fantasies into concrete burning desires or vanquish any existing unreal illusions.

Ideally I would further advise that if you could arrange this sort of experience just once every year or more, you will have done your child so much good, they can never finish thanking you for it – because by the end of it all, you would have weeded out unstable fantasies and established full blown desires they can reliably travel into the future with. You see, in the book of Genesis 1, we are made aware God created everything *"after their kind"* and the truth is, where the journey of life is concerned, no one ever travels satisfied, unless they are doing so *"with their kind."* There is a sort of spiritual magnet in every created being that connects him/her to his/her. It doesn't take revelation or prayer or study – you will just know, when you finally find your kind. It is on this basis that I recommend this sort of *"familiarisation"* tour of vocations, because if it is done well, your child will find the people *"of his kind."*

Align Intuitive and Educational Strengths

Finally, but by no means least, you do need to monitor very closely for each child, how their natural characters and abilities *(and the signals you inferred from them)* are aligning well with the educational subject areas they seem to be developing strengths in. There does need to be some form of harmony between the two. In other words, the subjects your child has greatest strengths in and the signals you infer from them must be coherent with the sense of direction you seemingly get, when considering their natural characters, ability and dispensations.

The readings on the child's inherent abilities compass must not show a different direction to the readings from the educational compass. If you are wondering if this has any Biblical basis to it, here is one in *2 Corinthians 13:1* which says *"...by the mouth of two or three witnesses every word shall be established."* The word *"mouth"* in the verse can also refer to *"source"* and the word *"witnesses"* could equally refer to *"occurrences"*. Hence effectively, the same verse could have read *""...from the sources of two or three occurrences, every word shall be established."* Read this way, the verse can now also be equally applied to non-human descriptions.

6

20 **PATRIARCH** PRAYERS FOR CHILDREN

In this last chapter, I list down about twenty powerful blessings and prayers that patriarchs, matriarchs and great men of old prayed for themselves, their children, their followers, their servants or their nations, which positively impacted their lives and those of their descendants even to this very generation. I have also provided the verses in the Bible where they can be found in the event that you wish to read further about the circumstances leading to such prayers. I have reformed the verses into prayers that can be made over your child immediately *(without changing much of the verse's content)*. For ease of use, I have also included blank spaces that you can simply insert your child's full name in, when praying. I have often found it useful to select one prayer for every month (or two short ones). That way, I would have intensively deposited each prayer over the life and into the destinies of my children.

Here is a peculiar truth I am sure you already know: As parents, God has given us a unique grace to deploy our voices into the future of our children. In a way, we can send our voice ahead of them, like John the Baptist, to level the hills ahead of them and fill the valleys they would have otherwise stumble into even before they arrive into twenty or so years in the future – that I'd say, is phenomenal grace.

Believe this one thing as you utilise these prayers – the word of God on its own *(without any other help)*, has enough power to accomplish all things it is deployed for. As you pray these prayers over your child, I ask the Spirit of God to move through your breath and impact your child permanently – for the words, which you will now speak, they are Spirit and they are life.

(1) Genesis 1:28

"According to the very word of Jehovah God Almighty, I bless ------- to be fruitful and to multiply; to fill the earth and subdue it; have dominion over the fish of the sea, over the birds of the air, over every living thing that moves on the earth and everything spiritually and physically represented by the fish of the sea, birds of the air and living things on the earth."

(2) Genesis 24:60 (Only for GIRL child)

"My daughter -------, may you become the mother of thousands of ten thousands; and may your descendants possess the gates of those who hate them in the mighty name of Jesus the Christ, of Nazareth."

(3) Exodus 33:13

"Now therefore, I pray O God of my father Abraham, Isaac and Jacob, if I have found favour in Your sight, show ------- Your way in all things, that *s/he* may know You early and that *s/he* may find favour in Your sight. And consider that *s/he* is Your people."

(4) Exodus 33:15

"Merciful God of Israel, You who showed mercy to Your prophet Moses, if Your Presence does not go with -------, then I pray thee, do not bring ------- up from here. For how then will it be known that ------- has found favour in Your sight, except You go with *him/her*?"

---

(5) Numbers 6:24-26 (important to lay right hand on child)

"-------, the Lord bless you and keep you; the Lord make His face shine upon you and be gracious to you; the Lord lift up His countenance upon you, and give you peace."

---

(6) Deuteronomy 3:24-25

'O Lord God, You have begun to show ------- Your greatness and Your mighty hand, for what god is there in heaven or on earth who can do anything like Your works and Your mighty deeds? I pray thee, order the steps of ------- and take away error from *her/his* path, that *s/he* may accomplish *her/his* destiny, in *her/his* lifetime. In the name of Jesus the Christ, of Nazareth."

---

(7) Deuteronomy 28:3-5

"-------, by my legal prophetic authority over your life, I decree blessed shall you be in the city, and blessed shall you be in the country. Blessed shall be the fruit of your body, the produce of your ground and the increase of your herds, the increase of your cattle and the offspring of your flocks. "Blessed shall be your basket and your kneading bowl all the days of your life and your descendants."

(8) 1 Samuel 2:1-3

"In the name of Jesus the Christ, I decree over your life -------; your heart will always rejoice in the Lord and your horns shall be exalted in Him. May you smile at your enemies, because you rejoice in the salvation of the Lord."

(9) 1 Samuel 26:25

"May you be blessed, my *son/daughter* -------! You shall both do great things and also still prevail."

(10) 2 Kings 6:17

"LORD, by the power of your Spirit, I pray, open the eyes of my *daughter/son* ------- that s/he may see."

(11) 1 Chronicles 4:10

"O God of Israel, I call on You, that You would bless ------- indeed, and enlarge *her/his* territory, that Your hand would be with *her/him*, and that You would keep *her/him* from evil, that *s/he* may not cause or be caused pain!"

(12) 1 Chronicles 29:19

"God of David, I pray thee, give my *daughter/son* ------- a loyal heart to keep Your commandments and Your testimonies and Your statutes, to do all these things in the entirety of *her/his* life."

(13) Job 29:5-8

"Almighty God of Job, creator of heaven and earth, I call on You. Be with -------, throughout *her/his* life; Let *her/his* children be around *her/him*; let *her/his* steps be bathed with butter, and the rocks pour out rivers of oil for *her/him*! When *s/he* goes out to the gate by the city and takes *her/his* seat in the open square, let the young men see *her/him* and hide and the aged rise and stand. In Jesus' Mighty name."

(14) Psalm 1: 1 – 3

"Oh God of David, bless my *daughter/son* ------- so *s/he* does not walk in the counsel of the ungodly, nor stand in the path of sinners, nor sit in the seat of the scornful; but I beseech thee O Lord, let *her/his* delight be in Your word and on it let *her/him* meditate day and night. According Lord, reward my *daughter/son* ------- to be like a tree planted by the rivers of water, that brings forth its fruit in its season, whose leaf also shall not wither; and whatever *s/he* does, let it prosper. In Jesus' mighty name."

(15) Psalm 23

"------- by my prophetic mandate over your life; I decree the Lord shall be your shepherd and you shall never lack. He shall rest you in green pastures and refresh you always. He'll restore your soul and lead you in His path of righteousness. When you walk through the darkness of this world, you will not fear any evil, for my God shall be with you; His rod and staff shall comfort you. God in heaven will bless and anoint you exceedingly in the presence of your enemies. I declare over your life -------, that the goodness and mercies of My God, shall follow you all the days of your life; and your feet shall never depart from the house of God"

---

(16) Psalm 112

"O God, who made heaven and earth, I pray thee; when my *daughter/son* ------- lifts up *her/his* eyes to You, may you come down to *her/his* help. Because You do not slumber Lord, may You not permit *her/his* foot to be moved. -------, I affirm the word of God over your life; the sun shall not strike you by day, nor the moon by night; the Lord shall preserve you from all evil; He shall preserve your soul. The Lord shall preserve your going out and your coming in now and forevermore."

---

(17) Psalm 118: 15 – 17

"In the name of Jesus the Christ, I pray for you, -------; may the voice of rejoicing and salvation remain in your home always; may the right hand of the Lord do valiantly on your behalf. May the right hand of the Lord be exalted upon you; may the right hand of the Lord do valiantly for you. You shall not die, but live, and declare all the works of the Lord in your life"

(18) Nehemiah 13:14

"Remember O my God, concerning ------- and do not wipe out *her/his* good deeds that *s/he* has done for the house of God, and for its services!"

(19) Habakkuk 3:19

"-------, The Lord God is your strength; He will make your feet like deer's feet, and He will make you walk on your high hills. In the name of Jesus the Christ."

(20) 3 John 1:2

"I pray above all, that you -------, may prosper in all things and be in excellent health all the days of your life, just as your soul prospers, by the transforming power of the Blood of Jesus the Christ, the son of the most high God."

AUTHOR'S OTHER WORKS

Title: Is This Why Africa Is? (E-book & Paperback)
Description: I ask all the questions about Africa that nobody else will. Deep, profound questions
Availability: Amazon & Kindle
Link to View: http://goo.gl/ecRMig

Title: Where Did God Hide His Diamonds? (E-book & Paperback)
Description: Discovering what exactly God has hidden in you, finding it & prospering freely from it
Availability: Amazon & Kindle
Link to View: http://goo.gl/ecRMig

Title: Doing Business with God (E-book & Paperback)
Description: 60 shocking biblical principles for extraordinary leadership, business and politics.
Availability: Amazon & Kindle
Link to View: http://goo.gl/ecRMig

Title: Midnight Philosophies (E-book & Paperback)
Description: My Deep thoughts, Philosophies, Reflections – Whispers of my mind.
Availability: Amazon & Kindle
Link to View: http://goo.gl/ecRMig

Title:	This Godly Child of Mine (E-book & Paperback)
Description:	A revelatory book on how to raise godly children in a perverse and lawless world
Availability:	Amazon & Kindle
Link to View:	http://goo.gl/ecRMig

Title:	The Deputy Minister for Corruption (E-book & Paperback)
Description:	A Novel
Availability:	Amazon & Kindle
Link to View:	http://goo.gl/ecRMig

Title:	A Dove in the Storm (E-book & Paperback)
Description:	A Novel
Availability:	Amazon & Kindle
Link to View:	http://goo.gl/ecRMig

Title:	100% JOB INTERVIEW SUCCESS (E-book & Paperback)
Description:	A simple, straightforward guide to passing every job interview you attend.
Availability:	Amazon & Kindle
Link to View:	http://goo.gl/ecRMig

Title:	Bible-by-Heart (Mobile App)
Description:	A simple but effective App to help anyone memorize 500 Bible verses in a year.
Availability:	iTunes & Google Play Stores

Link to View:	http://goo.gl/T3UdPN (i-Tunes)
Link to View:	http://goo.gl/ljnECR (Android)

Title:	Holy Rat (Mobile Game)
Description:	An exciting Christian mobile game that unwittingly gets you addicted to the word.
Availability:	iTunes & Google Play Stores
Link to View:	http://goo.gl/bygjBi (i-Tunes)
Link to View:	http://goo.gl/F18RM0 (Android)

ABOUT THE AUTHOR

Marricke Kofi GANE, is a gifted African Author, Philosopher, Public Speaker, Coach and Educationist. His writings carry real depth, are highly motivating yet challenging every status quo. He displays dexterity of mind and refined humour where appropriate. He is never shy in some of his works, to show a strong balance between his Christian roots and the reality of living in today's world.

Discover for yourself, all that his writings stand for - to dare, to motivate, to impact!! For more on him, visit www.marrickekofigane.com

Dear Reader,

Thank you for reading this book. I am hopeful that the information provided in it has given you some new learning, challenged you, or provided some answers and inspiration.

I respectfully ask your indulgence in 2 simple ways:

1. Whatever positive action(s) this book has inspired you to take, DO IT NOW. Not later.

2. Help other potential readers who without you, may never read this book by simply following the link below to leave a review. It only takes 3 minutes, but it could be a lifetime blessing for someone out there.

    http://goo.gl/v03bu2

Thank you once again for everything

Marricke Kofi GANE

www.ingramcontent.com/pod-product-compliance
Lightning Source LLC
Chambersburg PA
CBHW071859020426
42331CB00010B/2589